Ron gives us a perspective on living through insightful and moving short stories, humorous anecdotes, and a simple belief in the good we all possess but seem to have forgotten.

Ron's book should be mandatory reading for the human race. This book will make you believe in something greater than us even if you are not religious.

—Craig Dean, U.S. Navy Seal, Retired,
president, C.D.M. Development

Ron Dykstra has been making me laugh for almost forty years! He has a gift: the ability to see the truth and humor in everyday life. His collection of stories will warm your heart and put a smile in your life.

—Joe Pollock, national sales manager,
retired, ford industries

This is one of the most creative and well organized books that I have ever read. I am so impressed with Ron's book: its never compromising standards; spiritual values; and good, clean jokes and heartfelt stories. I could not put the book down.

—Larry Stith, commercial real estate broker

CLEAN JOKES

INSPIRATIONAL STORIES AND MORE

CLEAN JOKES

INSPIRATIONAL STORIES AND MORE

A COLLECTION BY

RON DYKSTRA

Tate Publishing & *Enterprises*

Published by Tate Publishing & Enterprises, LLC
127 E. Trade Center Terrace | Mustang, Oklahoma 73064 USA
1.888.361.9473 | www.tatepublishing.com

Tate Publishing is committed to excellence in the publishing industry. The company reflects the philosophy established by the founders, based on Psalm 68:11,
"The Lord gave the word and great was the company of those who published it."

Cover design by Cole Roberts
Interior design by Stephanie Woloszyn

Published in the United States of America

ISBN: 978-1-60799-856-3
Humor / Form / Anecdotes
09.07.28

**DEDICATED TO MY BEAUTIFUL,
SUPPORTIVE WIFE LISA,**

MY WONDERFUL SON JONATHAN,

**AND ALL OF MY FRIENDS
WHO LAUGHED, CRIED,
AND WERE MY BEST CRITICS.**

We are not human beings going through a
temporary spiritual experience,
We are spiritual beings going through a
temporary human experience.
Have a great day and bless someone else
in some little way today! God is so good!

Give me a sense of humor, Lord,
Give me the grace to see a joke,
To get some humor out of life,
And pass it on to other folk!

LAURA LOU

A guy was sitting quietly reading his paper when his wife walked up behind him and whacked him on the head with a magazine.

"What was that for?" he asked.

"That was for the piece of paper in your pants pocket with the name Laura Lou written on it," she replied.

"Two weeks ago when I went to the races, Laura Lou was the name of one of the horses I bet on," he explained.

"Oh honey, I'm sorry," she said. "I should have known there was a good explanation."

Three days later he was watching a ball game on TV when she walked up and hit him in the head again, this time with the iron skillet, which knocked him out cold.

When he came to, he asked, "What was that for?"

She replied... "Your horse called."

THE GIFT

A young man was getting ready to graduate from college. For many months he had admired a beautiful sports car in a dealer's showroom, and knowing his father could well afford it, he told him that was all he wanted. As graduation day approached, the young man awaited signs that his father had purchased the car.

Finally, on the morning of his graduation, his father called him into his private study. His father told him how proud he was to have such a fine son, and told him how much he loved him. He handed his son a beautifully wrapped gift box. Curious, but somewhat disappointed, the young man opened the box and found a lovely, leather-bound Bible with the young man's name embossed in gold.

Angrily, he raised his voice to his father and said, "With all your money, you give me a Bible?"

He stormed out of the house, leaving the Bible.

Many years passed, and the young man was very successful in business. He had a beautiful home and wonderful family, but he realized his father was very old. He thought perhaps he should go to him. He had not seen him since that graduation day. Before he could make arrangements, he received a telegram telling him his father had passed away and willed all of his possessions to his son. He needed to come home immediately and take care of things.

When he arrived at his father's house, sudden sadness and regret filled his heart. He began to search through his father's important papers and saw the still-new Bible, just as he had left it years ago. With tears, he opened the Bible and began to turn the pages. His father had carefully underlined a verse, Matt 7:11, "And if ye, being evil know how to give good gifts to your children, how much more shall your Heavenly father which is in heaven, give to those who ask Him?"

As he read those words, a car key dropped from the back of the Bible. It had a tag with the dealer's name, the same dealer who had the sports car he had desired. On the tag was the date of his graduation, and the words ... *paid in full.*

How many times do we miss God's blessings because they are not packaged as we expected? Do not spoil what you have by desiring what you have not; but remember that what you now have was once among the things you only hoped for ...

Jesus loves you!

ONLY GREAT MINDS CAN READ THIS . . . THIS IS WEIRD, BUT INTERESTING!

Fi yuo can raed this, yuo have a sgtrane mind too!

Can yuo raed this? Olny 55 plepoe out of 100 can.

I cdnuolt blveiee taht I cluod aulaclty uesdnatnrd waht I was rdanieg. The phaonmneal pweor of the hmuan mnid, aoccdrnig to a reeasrch at Cmabrigde Uinervtisy, it dseno't mtaetr in waht oerdr the ltteres in a wrod are, the olny iproamtnt tihng is taht the frsit and lsat ltteer be in the rghit pclae. The rset can be a taotl mses and you can sitll raed it whotuit a pboerlm. Tihs is bcuseae the huamn mnid deos not raed ervey lteter by istlef, but the wrod as a wlohe. Azanmig huh? Yaeh and I awlyas tghuhot slpeling was ipmorantt!!

WILL YOU MARRY ME ?

There was a blind girl who hated herself because she was blind. She hated everyone, except her loving boyfriend. He was always there for her. She told her boyfriend, "If I could only see the world, I would marry you."

One day, someone donated a pair of eyes to her. When the bandages came off, she was able to see everything, including her boyfriend.

He asker her, "Now that you can see the world, will you marry me?"

The girl looked at her boyfriend and saw that he was blind. The sight of his closed eyelids shocked her. She hadn't expected that. The thought of looking at them the rest of her life led her to refuse to marry him. Her boyfriend left in tears and days later had a note written to her saying:

"Take good care of your eyes, my dear, for before they were yours, they were mine."

PEANUTS

A tour bus driver is driving with a busload of seniors down the highway when he is tapped on his shoulder by a little old lady. She offers him a handful of peanuts, which he gratefully munches up.

After about fifteen minutes, she taps him on the shoulder again. She hands him another handful of peanuts.

She repeats this gesture about five more times.

When she is about to hand him another batch again, he asks the little old lady, "Why don't you eat the peanuts yourself?"

"We can't chew them because we've no teeth," she replied.

The puzzled driver asks, "Why do you buy them, then?"

The old lady replied, "We just love the chocolate."

FORREST GUMP GOES TO HEAVEN

The day finally arrives. Forrest Gump dies and goes to heaven. He is at the pearly gates, met by St. Peter himself. However, the gates are closed, and Forrest approaches the gatekeeper.

St. Peter said, "Well, Forrest, it is certainly good to see you. We have heard a lot about you. I must tell you, though, that the place is filling up fast, and we have been administering an entrance examination for everyone. The test is short, but you have to pass it before you can get into heaven."

Forrest responds, "It sure is good to be here, St. Peter, sir. But nobody ever told me about any entrance exam. I sure hope that the test ain't too hard. Life was a big enough test as it was."

St. Peter continued, "Yes, I know, Forrest, but the test is only three questions.

First:

What two days of the week begin with the letter T?

Second:

How many seconds are there in a year?

Third:

What is God's first name?"

Forrest leaves to think the questions over. He returns the next day and sees St. Peter, who waves him up and says,

"Now that you have had a chance to think the questions over, tell me your answers."

Forrest replied, "Well, the first one–which two days in the week begins with the letter T.

Shucks, that one is easy. That would be today and tomorrow."

The saint's eyes opened wide and he exclaimed, "Forrest, that is not what I was thinking, but you do have a point, and I guess I did not specify, so I will give you credit for that answer.

"How about the next one?" asked St. Peter. "How many seconds in a year?"

"Now that one is harder," replied Forrest, "but I thunk and thunk about that, and I guess the only answer can be twelve."

Astounded, St. Peter said, "Twelve? Twelve? Forrest, how in heaven's name could you come up with twelve seconds in a year?"

Forrest replied, "Shucks, there's got to be twelve: January 2nd, February 2nd, March 2nd ..."

"Hold it," interrupts St. Peter. "I see where you are going with this, and I see your point, though that was not quite what I had in mind... But I will have to give you credit for that one, too. Let us go on with the third and final question. Can you tell me God's first name?"

"Sure," Forrest replied, "it's Andy."

"Andy?" exclaimed an exasperated and frustrated St. Peter. "Okay, I can understand how you came up with your answers to my first two questions, but just how in the world did you come up with the name Andy as the first name of God?"

"Shucks, that was the easiest one of all," Forrest replied. "I learnt it from the song:

'Andy walks with me, Andy talks with me, Andy tells me I am his own.'"

St. Peter opened the pearly gates, and said: "Run, Forrest, run."

A DOG NAMED LUCKY

Mary and her husband Jim had a dog named "Lucky." Lucky was a real character. Whenever Mary and Jim had company come for a weekend visit, they would warn their friends not to leave their luggage open, because Lucky would help himself to whatever struck his fancy. Inevitably, someone would forget and something would come up missing.

Mary or Jim would go to Lucky's toy box in the basement and there the treasure would be, amid all of Lucky's other favorite toys. Lucky always stashed his finds in his toy box, and he was very particular that his toys stay in the box.

It happened that Mary found out she had breast cancer. Something told her she was going to die of this disease. In fact, she was just sure it was fatal. She scheduled the double mastectomy, fear riding her shoulders. The night before she was to go to the hospital she cuddled with Lucky. A thought struck her... what would happen to Lucky?

Although the three-year-old dog liked Jim, he was Mary's dog through and through. *If I die, Lucky will be abandoned,* Mary thought. *He won't understand that I didn't want to leave him.* The thought made her sadder than thinking of her own death.

The double mastectomy was harder on Mary than her doctors had anticipated and Mary was hospitalized for over two weeks. Jim took Lucky for his evening walk faithfully, but the little dog just drooped, whining and acting miserable.

Finally the day came for Mary to leave the hospital. When she arrived home, Mary was so exhausted she couldn't even make it up the steps to her bedroom. Jim made his wife comfortable on the couch and left her to nap. Lucky stood watching Mary, but he didn't come to her when she called. It made Mary sad, but sleep soon overcame her and she dozed.

When Mary woke for a second, she couldn't understand what was wrong. She couldn't move her head and her body felt heavy and hot. But panic soon gave way to laughter when Mary realized the problem. She was covered, literally blanketed, with every treasure Lucky owned! While she had slept, the sorrowing dog had made trip after trip to the basement bringing his beloved mistress all his favorite things in life. He had covered her with his love.

Mary forgot about dying. Instead she and Lucky began living again, walking further and further together every day. It's been twelve years now and Mary is still cancer-free. Lucky? He still steals treasures and stashes them in his toy box, but Mary remains his greatest treasure.

Remember, live every day to the fullest. Each minute is a blessing. And never forget the people who make a difference in our lives are not the ones with the most credentials, the most money, or the most awards. They are the ones that care for us. If you see someone without a smile today, give them one of yours!

Live simply. Love seriously. Care deeply. Speak kindly. Leave the rest to God…

LIFE IS A GIFT

Today, before you say an unkind word,
think of someone who can't speak...

Before you complain about the taste of your food,
think of someone who has nothing to eat...

Before you complain about your husband or wife,
think about someone who's crying out to God for a companion...

Today, before you complain about life,
think of someone who went too early to heaven.

Before whining about the distance you drive,
think of someone who walks the same distance with their feet.

And, when you are tired and complain about your job,
think of the unemployed, the disabled, and those who wish they had your job.

And, when depressing thoughts seem to get you down,
put a smile on your face and think:

You're alive and still around...

THE INTERVIEW

The FBI had an opening for an assassin. After all the background checks, interviews and testing were done, there were three finalists: two men and a woman. For the final test, the FBI agents took one of the men to a large metal door and handed him a gun.

"We must know that you will follow our instructions no matter what the circumstances. Inside the room you will find your wife sitting in a chair. Kill her!"

The man said, "You can't be serious. I could never shoot my wife."

The agent said, "Then you're not the right man for this job. Take your wife and go home."

The second man was given the same instructions. He took the gun and went into the room. All was quiet for about five minutes.

The man came out with tears in his eyes.

"I tried, but I can't kill my wife."

The agent said, "You don't have what it takes. Take your wife home."

Finally, it was the woman's turn. She was given the same instructions to kill her husband. She took the gun and went into the room. Shots were heard, one after another.

They heard screaming, crashing, and banging on the walls. After a few minutes, all was quiet. The door opened slowly and there stood the woman, wiping the sweat from her brow.

"This gun is loaded with blanks," she said. "I had to beat him to death with the chair."

THE RAFFLE

Young Chuck moved to Texas and bought a donkey from a farmer for $100.00. The farmer agreed to deliver the donkey the next day. The next day he drove up and said, "Sorry son, but I have some bad news. The donkey died."

Chuck replied, "Well, then just give me my money back."

The farmer said, "Can't do that. I went and spent it already."

Chuck said, "Okay, then, just bring me the dead donkey."

The farmer asked, "What ya gonna do with him?"

Chuck said, "I'm going to raffle him off."

The farmer said, "You can't raffle off a dead donkey."

Chuck said, "Sure I can. Watch me. I just won't tell anybody he's dead."

A month later, the farmer met up with Chuck and asked, "What happened to that dead donkey?"

Chuck said, "I raffled him off. I sold 500 tickets at two dollars a piece and made a profit of $898.00."

The farmer said, "Didn't anyone complain?"

Chuck said, "Just the guy who won. So I gave him his two dollars back."

Chuck now works for the government!

SAYING GRACE

Last week, I took my children to a restaurant.

My six-year-old son asked if he could say grace.

As we bowed our heads he said, "God is good, God is great. Thank you for the food, and I would even thank you more if Mom gets us ice cream for dessert. And liberty and justice for all! Amen!"

Along with the laughter from the other customers nearby, I heard a woman remark, "That's what's wrong with this country. Kids today don't even know how to pray. Asking God for ice cream! Why, I never!"

Hearing this, my son burst into tears and asked me, "Did I do it wrong? Is God mad at me?"

As I held him and assured him that he had done a terrific job and that God was certainly not mad at him, an elderly gentleman approached the table.

He winked at my son and said, "I happen to know that God thought that was a great prayer."

"Really?" my son asked.

"Cross my heart," the man replied.

Then, in a theatrical whisper, he added (indicating the woman whose remark had started this whole thing), "Too bad she never asks God for ice cream. A little ice cream is good for the soul sometimes."

Naturally, I bought my kids ice cream at the end of the meal. My son stared at his for a moment, and then did something I will remember for the rest of my life.

He picked up his sundae and, without a word, walked over and placed it in front of the woman. With a big smile he told her, "Here, this is for you. Ice cream is good for the soul sometimes; and my soul is good already."

WHEN I SAY I'M BROKE . . . I'M BROKE!

A little old lady answered a knock on the door one day, only to be confronted by a well-dressed young man carrying a vacuum cleaner.

"Good morning," said the young man. "If I could take a couple of minutes of your time, I would like to demonstrate the very latest in high-powered vacuum cleaners."

"Go away," said the old lady. "I haven't got any money, I'm broke!"

As she proceeded to close the door, the young man wedged his foot in the door and pushed it wide open.

"Don't be too hasty," he said. "Not until you have at least seen my demonstration."

And with that, he emptied a bucket of horse manure on her hallway carpet.

"If this vacuum cleaner does not remove all traces of this horse manure from your carpet, Madam, I will personally eat the remainder."

The old lady stepped back and said, "Well, I hope you've got a good appetite, because they cut off my electricity this morning."

WISDOM

1. Don't worry about what people think; they don't do it very often.
2. Going to church doesn't make you a Christian any more than standing in a garage makes you a car.
3. Artificial intelligence is no match for natural stupidity.
4. Not one shred of evidence supports the notion that life is serious.
5. A person who is nice to you but rude to the waiter is not a nice person.
6. For every action, there is an equal and opposite government program.
7. If you look like your passport picture, you probably need a trip.
8. Bills travel through the mail at twice the speed of checks.
9. A conscience is what hurts when all of your other parts feel so good.
10. Eat well, stay fit, die anyway.
11. Men are from earth. Women are from earth. Deal with it.

12. No man has ever been shot while doing dishes.
13. A balanced diet is a cookie in each hand.
14. Middle age is when broadness of the mind and narrowness of the waist change places.
15. Opportunities always look bigger after they have passed.
16. Junk is something you've kept for years and throw away three weeks before you need it.
17. There is always one more imbecile than you counted on.
18. Experience is a wonderful thing. It enables you to recognize a mistake when you make it again.
19. By the time you can make ends meet, they move the ends.
20. Thou shalt not weigh more than thy refrigerator.
21. Someone who thinks logically provides a nice contrast to the real world.
22. It isn't the jeans that make your butt look fat.
23. There is a very fine line between "hobby" and "mental illness."
24. People who want to share their religious views with you almost never want you to share yours with them.
25. You should not confuse your career with your life.

26. Nobody cares if you can't dance well. Just get up and dance.

27. Never lick a steak knife.

28. The most destructive force in the universe is gossip.

29. You will never find anybody who can give you a clear and compelling reason why we observe daylight savings time.

30. You should never say anything to a woman that even remotely suggests that you think she's pregnant unless you can see an actual baby emerging from her at that moment.

31. The one thing that unites all human beings, regardless of age, gender, religion, economic status, or ethnic background, is that, deep down inside, we *all* believe that we are above average drivers.

32. Your friends love you anyway.

33. How old would you be if you didn't know how old you are?

34. Never, under any circumstances, take a laxative and a sleeping pill on the same night.

THOUGHT FOR THE DAY:

Never be afraid to try something new.

Remember that a lone amateur built the ark.

A large group of professionals built the Titanic.

HEY, FRIEND!

An elderly Chinese woman had two large pots, each hung on the ends of a pole that she carried across her neck.

One of the pots had a crack in it, while the other pot was perfect and always delivered a full portion of water.

At the end of the long walks from the stream to the house, the cracked pot arrived only half-full.

For a full two years, this went on daily, with the woman bringing home only one and a half pots of water.

Of course, the perfect pot was proud of its accomplishments. But the poor cracked pot was ashamed of its own imperfection, and miserable that it could only do half of what it had been made to do.

After two years of what it perceived to be bitter failure, it spoke to the woman one day by the stream.

"I am ashamed of myself, because this crack in my side causes water to leak out all the way back to your house."

The old woman smiled.

"Did you notice that there are flowers on your side of the path, but not on the other pot's side? That's because I have always known about your flaw, so I planted flower seeds on your side of the path, and every day while we walk back, you water them. For two years I have been able to pick these beautiful flowers to decorate the table. Without you being just the way you are, there would not be this beauty to grace the house."

Each of us has our own unique flaw. But it's the cracks

and flaws we each have that make our lives together so very interesting and rewarding.

You've just got to take each person for what they are and look for the good in them.

So, to all of my crackpot friends, have a great day and remember to smell the flowers on your side of the path!

CYANIDE

A nice, calm, and respectable lady went into the pharmacy, walked up to the pharmacist, looked straight into his eyes, and said, "I would like to buy some cyanide."

The pharmacist asked, "Why in the world do you need cyanide?"

The lady replied, "I need it to poison my husband."

The pharmacist's eyes got big and he exclaimed, "Lord have mercy! I can't give you cyanide to kill your husband. That's against the law! I'll lose my license! They'll throw both of us in jail! All kinds of bad things will happen. Absolutely not! You can not have any cyanide!"

The lady reached into her purse and pulled out a picture of her husband in bed with the pharmacist's wife. The pharmacist looked at the picture and replied, "Well, now, that's different. You didn't tell me you had a prescription."

FEMALE DRIVER

I was riding to work yesterday when I observed a female driver cut right in front of a pickup truck, causing the pickup driver to drive onto the shoulder of the road to avoid hitting her.

This evidently angered the driver enough that he hung his arm out the window and shook his fist in a threatening way at her. *Man, that guy is stupid,* I thought to myself.

I *always* smile nicely and wave in a sheepish manner whenever a female does anything to me in traffic, and here's why:

I drive forty-eight miles each way every day to work. That's ninety-six miles each day. Of those, sixteen miles each way is bumper-to-bumper. Most of the bumper-to-bumper traffic is on an eight-lane highway. There are seven cars every forty feet for thirty-two miles.

That works out to 982 cars every mile, or 31,424 cars.

Even though the rest of the thirty-two miles is not bumper-to-bumper, I figure I pass at least another 4,000 cars.

That brings the number to something like 36,000 cars that I pass every day.

Statistically, females drive half of these. That's 18,000 woman drivers!

In any given group of females, 1 in 28 has PMS.

That's 642.

According to *Cosmopolitan* magazine, 70% describe their love life as dissatisfying or unrewarding.

That's 449.

According to the National Institute of Health, 22% of all females have seriously considered suicide or homicide.

That's 98.

And 34% describe men as their biggest problem.

That's 33.

According to the National Rifle Association, 5% of all females carry weapons, and this number is increasing.

That means that *every single day,* I drive past at least one female that has a lousy love life, thinks men are her biggest problem, has seriously considered suicide or homicide, has PMS, and is armed.

Give her a threatening gesture?

I don't think so...

JUST STAY

A nurse took the tired, anxious serviceman to the bedside.

"Your son is here," she said to the old man.

She had to repeat the words several times before the patient's eyes opened. He was heavily sedated because of the pain of his heart attack. He dimly saw the young, uniformed marine standing outside the oxygen tent. He reached out his hand. The marine wrapped his toughened fingers around the old man's limp ones, squeezing a message of love and encouragement.

The nurse brought a chair so that the marine could sit beside the bed.

All through the night, the young marine sat there in the poorly lighted ward, holding the old man's hand and offering him words of love and strength.

Occasionally, the nurse suggested that the marine move away and rest awhile.

He refused.

Whenever the nurse came into the ward, the marine was oblivious of her and of the night noises of the hospital—the clanging of the oxygen tank, the laughter of the night staff members exchanging greetings, the cries and moans of the other patients.

Now and then she heard him say a few gentle words. The dying man said nothing, only held tightly to his son all through the night.

Along toward dawn, the old man died.

The marine released the now lifeless hand he had been holding and went to tell the nurse. While she did what she had to do, he waited.

Finally, she returned. She started to offer words of sympathy, but the marine interrupted her.

"Who was that man?" he asked.

The nurse was startled.

"He was your father," she answered.

"No, he wasn't," the marine replied. "I never saw him before in my life."

"Then why didn't you say something when I took you to him?"

"I knew right away there had been a mistake, but I also knew he needed his son, and his son just wasn't here. When I realized that he was too sick to tell whether or not I was his son, knowing how much he needed me, I stayed."

The next time someone needs you ... just be there.

Just stay ...

WHAT HAPPENED?

While walking down the street one day, a US senator was tragically hit by a truck and dies.

His soul arrived in heaven and was met by St. Peter at the entrance.

"Welcome to heaven," says St. Peter. Before you settle in, it seems there is a problem. We seldom see a high-ranking official around these parts, you see, so we're not sure what to do with you."

"No problem, just let me in," says the senator.

"Well, I'd like to, but I have orders from higher up. What we'll do is have you spend one day in hell and one in heaven. Then you can choose where to spend eternity."

"Really, I've made up my mind. I want to be in heaven," says the senator.

"I'm sorry, but we have our rules."

And with that, St. Peter escorts him to the elevator and he goes down, down, down to hell. The doors open and he finds himself in the middle of a green golf course. In the distance is a clubhouse and standing in front of it are all his friends and other politicians who had worked with him.

Everyone is very happy and in evening dress. They run to greet him, shake his hand, and reminisce about the good times they had while getting rich at the expense of the people.

They play a friendly game of golf and then dine on lobster, caviar, and champagne.

Also present is the devil, who really is a very friendly guy that has a good time dancing and telling jokes. They are having such a good time that before he realizes it, it is time to go.

Everyone gives him a hearty farewell and waves while the elevator rises.

The elevator goes up, up, up and the door reopens to heaven where St. Peter is waiting for him.

"Now it's time to visit heaven."

So, twenty-four hours pass with the senator joining a group of contented souls moving from cloud to cloud, playing the harp and singing. They have a good time and, before he realizes it, the twenty-four hours have gone by and St. Peter returns.

"Well, then, you've spent a day in hell and another in heaven. Now choose your eternity."

The senator reflects for a minute, then answers: "Well, I would never have said it before, I mean heaven has been delightful, but I think I would be better off in hell."

So St. Peter escorts him to the elevator and he goes down, down, down to hell.

Now the doors of the elevator open and he's in the middle of a barren land covered with waste and garbage.

He sees all his friends, dressed in rags, picking up the trash and putting it in black bags as more trash falls from above.

The devil comes over to him and puts his arm around his shoulder.

"I don't understand," stammers the senator. "Yesterday

I was here and there was a golf course and clubhouse, and we ate lobster and caviar, drank champagne, danced, and had a great time. Now there's just a wasteland full of garbage and my friends look miserable. What happened?"

The devil looks at him, smiles, and says…

"Yesterday we were campaigning. Today we voted."

TAXED TO DEATH

Tax his land,
Tax his bed,
Tax the table,
At which he's fed.

Tax his tractor,
Tax his mule,
Teach him taxes
Are the rule.

Tax his cow,
Tax his goat,
Tax his pants,
Tax his coat.

Tax his ties,
Tax his shirt,
Tax his work,
Tax his dirt.

Tax his tobacco,
Tax his drink,
Tax him if he
Tries to think.

Tax his cigars,
Tax his beers,
If he cries, then
Tax his tears.

Tax his car,
Tax his gas,
Find other ways
To tax his rear.

Tax all he has
Then let him know
That you won't be done
Till he has no dough.

When he screams and hollers,
Then tax him some more,
Tax him till
He's good and sore.

Then tax his coffin,
Tax his grave,
Tax the sod in
Which he's laid.

Put these words
Upon his tomb,
"Taxes drove me
to my doom."

When he's gone,
Do not relax,
It's time to apply
The inheritance tax.

TAXES, TAXES & MORE TAXES

Accounts Receivable Tax
Building Permit Tax
CDL License Tax
Cigarette Tax
Corporate Income Tax
Dog License Tax
Excise Taxes
Federal Income Tax
Federal Unemployment Tax (FUTA)
Fishing License Tax
Food License Tax
Fuel Permit Tax
Gasoline Tax
Gross Receipts Tax
Hunting License Tax
Inheritance Tax
Inventory Tax
IRS Interest Charges IRS Penalties (tax on top of tax)
Liquor Tax
Luxury Tax
Marriage License Tax
Medicare Tax
Personal Property Tax
Property Tax
Real Estate Tax
Service Charge Tax

Social Security Tax
Road Usage Tax
Sales Tax
Recreational Vehicle Tax
School Tax
State Income Tax
State Unemployment Tax (SUTA)
Telephone Federal Excise Tax
Telephone Federal Universal Service Fee Tax
Telephone Federal, State, and Local Surcharge Tax
Telephone Minimum Usage Surcharge Tax
Telephone Recurring and Non-Recurring Charges Tax
Telephone State and Local Tax
Telephone Usage Charge Tax
Utility Taxes
Vehicle License Registration Tax
Vehicle Sales Tax
Watercraft Registration Tax
Well Permit Tax
Worker's Compensation Tax

Still think this is funny?

Not one of these taxes existed 100 years ago, and our nation was the most prosperous in the world.

We had absolutely no national debt, had the largest middle class in the world, and Mom stayed home to raise the kids.

THE STRANGER

A few years after I was born, my Dad met a stranger who was new to our small Texas town. From the beginning, Dad was fascinated with this enchanting newcomer and soon invited him to live with our family. The stranger was quickly accepted and was around from then on.

As I grew up, I never questioned his place in my family. In my young mind, he had a special niche. My parents were complementary instructors: Mom taught me good from evil and Dad taught me to obey. But the stranger... he was our storyteller. He would keep us spellbound for hours on end with adventures, mysteries, and comedies.

If I wanted to know anything about politics, history, or science, he always knew the answers about the past, understood the present, and even seemed able to predict the future! He took my family to the first major league ball game. He made me laugh, and he made me cry.

The stranger never stopped talking, but Dad didn't seem to mind.

Sometimes, Mom would get up quietly while the rest of us were shushing each other to listen to what he had to say, and she would go to the kitchen for peace and quiet (I wonder now if she ever prayed for the stranger to leave).

Dad ruled our household with certain moral convictions, but the stranger never felt obligated to honor them.

Profanity, for example, was not allowed in our home ... not from us, our friends, or any visitors. Our longtime visitor, however, got away with four-letter words that burned my ears, made my Dad squirm, and my mother blush.

My Dad didn't permit the liberal use of alcohol. But the stranger encouraged us to try it on a regular basis. He made cigarettes look cool, cigars manly, and pipes distinguished. He talked freely (much too freely!) about sex. His comments were sometimes blatant, sometimes suggestive, and generally embarrassing.

I now know that my early concepts about relationships were influenced strongly by the stranger. Time after time, he opposed the values of my parents, yet he was seldom rebuked. And *never* asked to leave.

More than fifty years have passed since the stranger moved in with our family. He has blended right in and is not nearly as fascinating as he was at first. Still, if you would walk into my parents' den today, you would still find him sitting over in his corner, waiting for someone to listen to him talk and watch him draw his pictures. His name?

We just call him, "TV."

NOTE: This should be required reading for every household in America!

P.S. He has a wife now ... we call her "computer."

THE SUIT

A man who just died is delivered to a local mortuary wearing an expensive, expertly tailored black suit.

The female blonde mortician asks the deceased's wife how she would like the body dressed. She points out that the man does look good in the black suit he is already wearing.

The widow, however, says that she always thought her husband looked his best in blue, and that she wants him in a blue suit. She gives the blonde mortician a blank check and says, "I don't care what it costs, but please have my husband in a blue suit for the viewing."

The woman returns the next day for the wake. To her delight, she finds her husband dressed in a gorgeous blue suit with a subtle chalk stripe. The suit fits him perfectly.

She says to the mortician, "Whatever this costs, I'm very satisfied. You did an excellent job and I'm very grateful. How much did you spend?"

To her astonishment, the blonde mortician presents her with the blank check.

"There's no charge," she says.

"No, really, I must compensate you for the cost of that exquisite blue suit!" she says.

"Honestly, ma'am," the blonde says, "it cost nothing. You see, a deceased gentleman of about your husband's size was brought in shortly after you left yesterday, and he was wearing an attractive blue suit. I asked his wife if she minded him going to his grave wearing a black suit instead, and she said it made no difference as long as he looked nice.

So, I just switched the heads."

T.V. COMMERCIALS

A fifth grade teacher in a Christian school asked her class to look at TV commercials and see if they could use them in some way to communicate ideas about God.

Here are some of the results:

God is like
Bayer Aspirin.
He works miracles.

God is like
a Ford.
He's got a better idea.

God is like
Coke.
He's the real thing.

God is like
Hallmark Cards.
He cares enough to send the very best!

God is like
Tide.
He gets the stains out that others leave behind.

God is like
General Electric.
He brings good things to life.

God is like
Sears.
He has everything.

God is like
Alka-Seltzer.
Try him, you'll like him.

God is like
Scotch Tape.
You cant' see him, but you know he's there.

God is like
AllState.
You're in good hands with him.

God is like
VO-5 Hair Spray.
He holds through all kinds of weather.

God is like
Dial Soap
Aren't you glad you have him?
Don't you wish everybody did?

God is like
The U.S. Post Office
Neither rain, nor snow, nor sleet, nor ice will
keep him from his appointed destination.

God is like
Chevrolet.
The heartbeat of America.

God is like
Maxwell House.
Good to the last drop.

God is like
Bounty.
He is the quicker picker-upper,
can handle the tough jobs,
and he won't fall apart on you.

CAN I BORROW $25?

A man came home from work late, tired and irritated, to find his five-year-old son waiting for him at the door.

Son: Daddy, may I ask you a question?

Dad: Yeah, sure, what is it?

Son: Daddy, how much do you make an hour?

Dad: That's none of your business. Why do you ask such a thing?

Son: I just want to know. Please tell me, how much do you make an hour?

Dad: If you must know, I make $50 an hour.

Son: Oh. May I please borrow $25?

The father was furious. "If the only reason you asked that is so you can borrow some money to buy a silly toy or some other nonsense, then you march yourself straight to your room and go to bed. Think about why you are being so selfish. I don't work hard every day for such childish frivolities."

The little boy quietly went to his room and shut the door.

The man sat down and started to get even angrier about the little boy's question. How dare he ask such questions only to get some money! After about an hour or so, the man had calmed down and started to think:

maybe there was something he really needed to buy with that $25.00. He really doesn't ask for money very often.

The man went to the door of the little boy's room and opened the door.

Dad: Are you asleep, son?

Son: No, daddy, I'm awake.

Dad: I've been thinking, maybe I was too hard on you earlier. It's been a long day and I took out my aggravation on you. Here's the $25 you asked for.

The little boy sat straight up, smiling.

Son: Oh, thank you, Daddy.

The boy reached under his pillow and pulled out some crumpled up bills. When the man saw that the boy already had money he started to get angry again. The little boy slowly counted out his money and looked up at his father.

Dad: Why do you want more money if you already have some?

Son: Because I didn't have enough, but now I do. Can I buy an hour of your time? Please come home early tomorrow. I would like to have dinner with you.

The father was crushed. He put his arms around his little son, and he begged for his son's forgiveness. It's just a short reminder to all of you working so hard in life. We should not let time slip through our fingers without having spent some time with those who really matter to us, those close to our hearts. Do remember to share that $50 worth of your time with someone you love. If we die tomorrow, the company that we are working for could easily replace us in a matter of hours. But the family and friends we leave behind will feel the loss for the rest of their lives.

ITALIAN LOGIC

An old Italian Mafia "Don" is dying and he calls his grandson to his bed.

"Lissin-a me. I wanna for you to taka my chrome plated .38 revolver so you can always remember me."

"But Grampa, I really don't lika guns. Howz about you leava me your Rolex watch instead?"

"Shuddup an'a lissin. Somma day you gonna runna da business. You gonna have a beautifula wife, lotsa money, a bigga home, and maybe a couple of bambinos.

"Somma day you gonna comma home and maybe find your wife inna bed with another man. Whadda you gonna do then–pointa to you watch and say, *time's up?*"

WHO KNEW?

Eliminates ear mites: All it takes is a few drops of Wesson Corn Oil in your cat's ear. Massage it in, then clean with a cotton ball. Repeat daily for three days. The oil soothes the cat's skin, smothers the mites, and accelerates healing.

Kills fleas instantly: Dawn dishwashing liquid does the trick. Add a few drops to your dog's bath and shampoo the animal thoroughly. Rinse well to avoid skin irritations. Goodbye, fleas.

Rainy day cure for dog owners: Next time your dog comes in from the rain, simply wipe down the animal with Bounce or any dryer sheet, instantly making your dog smell springtime fresh.

DID YOU KNOW?

Drinking two glasses of Gatorade can relieve headache pain almost immediately—without the unpleasant side effects caused by traditional pain relievers.

Colgate toothpaste makes an excellent salve for burns.

Before you head to the drugstore for a high-priced inhaler filled with mysterious chemicals, try chewing on a couple of Curiously Strong Altoids Peppermints. They'll clear up your stuffed nose.

Achy muscles from a bout with the flu? Mix one tablespoon of horseradish in one cup of olive oil. Let the mixture sit for thirty minutes, then apply it as a massage oil for instant relief for aching muscles.

Sore throat? Just mix one fourth of a cup of vinegar with one fourth of a cup of honey and take one tablespoon six times a day. The vinegar kills the bacteria.

Cure urinary tract infections with Alka-Seltzer. Just dissolve two tablets in a glass of water and drink it at the onset of the symptoms. Alka-Seltzer begins eliminating urinary tract infections almost instantly—even though the product was never advertised for this use.

Honey remedy for skin blemishes: Cover the blemish with a dab of honey and place a Band-Aid over it. Honey kills the bacteria, keeps the skin sterile, and speeds healing. It works overnight.

Listerine therapy for toenail fungus: Get rid of unsightly toenail fungus by soaking your toes in Listerine mouthwash. The powerful antiseptic leaves your toenails looking healthy again.

Easy eyeglass protection: To prevent the screws in eyeglasses from loosening, apply a small drop of Maybelline Crystal Clear Nail Polish to the threads of the screws before tightening them.

Cleaning liquid that doubles as bug killer: If menacing bees, wasps, hornets, or yellow jackets get in your home and you can't find the insecticide, try a spray of Formula 409. Insects drop to the ground instantly.

Smart splinter remover: Just pour a drop of Elmer's Glue-All over the splinter, let dry, and peel the dried glue off the skin. The splinter sticks to the dried glue.

Hunt's Tomato Paste boil cure: Cover the boil with Hunt's Tomato Paste as a compress. The acids from the tomatoes soothe the pain and bring the boil to a head.

Balm for broken blisters: To disinfect a broken blister, dab a few drops of Listerine—a powerful antiseptic.

Vinegar to heal bruises: Soak a cotton ball in white vinegar and apply it to the bruise for one hour. The vinegar reduces the blueness and speeds up the healing process.

Quaker Oats for fast pain relief: It's not just for breakfast anymore! Mix two cups of Quaker Oats and one cup of water in a bowl and warm in the microwave for one minute. Cool slightly and apply mixture to your hands for soothing relief from arthritis pain.

THE DINNER

I was walking down the street when I was accosted by a particularly dirty and shabby-looking homeless woman who asked me for a couple of dollars for dinner.

I took out my wallet, got out ten dollars and asked, "If I give you this money, will you buy wine with it instead of dinner?

"No, I had to stop drinking years ago," the homeless woman told me.

"Will you use it to go shopping instead of buying food?" I asked.

"No, I don't waste time shopping," the homeless woman said. "I need to spend all my time trying to stay alive."

"Will you spend this on a beauty salon instead of food?" I asked.

"Are you *nuts!*" replied the homeless woman. "I haven't had my hair done in twenty years."

"Well," I said, "I'm not going to give you the money. Instead, I'm going to take you out for dinner with my husband and me tonight."

The homeless woman was shocked.

"Won't your husband be furious with you for doing that? I know I'm dirty, and probably smell pretty disgusting."

I said, "That's okay. It's important for him to see what a woman looks like after she has given up shopping, hair appointments, and wine."

DADDY'S DAY

Her hair was up in a ponytail,
Her favorite dress tied in a bow.
Today was Daddy's Day at school,
And she couldn't wait to go.

But her mommy tried to tell her,
That she probably should stay home.
Why the kids might not understand,
If she went to school alone.

But she was not afraid;
She knew just what to say.
What to tell her classmates,
Of why he wasn't there today.

But still her mother worried,
For her to face this day alone.
And that was why once again,
She tried to keep her daughter home.

But the girl went to school,
Eager to tell them all.
About a dad she never sees,
A dad who never calls.

There were daddies along the wall in back,
For everyone to meet.
Children squirming impatiently,
Anxious in their seats.

One by one the teacher called
A student from the class.
To introduce their daddy,
As seconds slowly passed.

At last the teacher called her name,
Every child turned to stare.
Each of them was searching,
For a man who wasn't there.

"Where's her daddy at?"
She heard a boy call out.
"She probably doesn't have one,"
Another student dared to shout.

And from somewhere near the back,
She heard a daddy say,
"Looks like another deadbeat dad,
Too busy to waste his day."

The words did not offend her,
As she smiled up at her Mom.
And looked back at her teacher,
Who told her to go on.

And with hands behind her back,
Slowly she began to speak.
And out of the mouth of a child,
Came words incredibly unique.

"My daddy couldn't be here,
Because he lives so far away.
But I know he wishes he could be,
Since this is such a special day.

And though you cannot meet him,
I wanted you to know.
All about my daddy,
And how much he loves me so.

He loved to tell me stories,
He taught me to ride a bike.
He surprised me with pink roses,
And taught me to fly a kite.

We used to share fudge sundaes,
And ice cream in a cone.
And though you cannot see him.
I'm not standing here alone.

Cause my daddy's always with me,
Even though we are apart.
I know because he told me,
He'll forever be in my heart."

With that, her little hand reached up,
And lay across her chest.
Feeling her own heartbeat.

And from somewhere here in the crowd of dads,
Her mother stood in tears.
Proudly watching her daughter,
Who was wise beyond her years.

For she stood up for the love
Of a man not in her life.
Doing what was best for her,
Doing what was right.

And when she dropped her hand back down,
Staring straight into the crowd.
She finished with a voice so soft,
But its message was clear and loud.

"I love my daddy very much,
He's my shining star.
And if he could, he'd be here,
But heaven's just too far.

You see he was a marine,
And died just this past year.
When a roadside bomb hit his convoy,
And taught Americans to fear.

But sometimes when I close my eyes,
It's like he never went away,"
And then she closed her eyes,
And saw him there that day.

And to her mother's amazement,
She witnessed with surprise.
A room full of daddies and children,
All starting to close their eyes.

Who knows what they saw before them,
Who knows what they felt inside.
Perhaps for merely a second,
They saw him at her side.

"I know you're with me, Daddy,"
To the silence she called out.
And what happened next made believers,
Of those once filled with doubt.

Not one in that room could explain it,
For each of their eyes had been closed.
But there on the desk beside her,
Was a fragrant long-stemmed pink rose.

And a child was blessed, if only for a moment,
By the love of her shining star.
And given the gift of believing,
That heaven is never too far.

They say it takes a minute to find a special person, an hour to appreciate them, a day to love them, but then an entire life to forget them.

Take the time ... to live and love, until eternity. God bless!

Please pray for our soldiers. It only takes a minute.

If it weren't for the United States military, there would be *no* United States of America ... Home of the free, because of the brave!

16 WIVES

A little boy was attending his first wedding.

After the service, his cousin asked him, "How many women can a man marry?"

"Sixteen," the boy responded. His cousin was amazed that he had an answer so quickly.

"How do you know that?"

"Easy," the little boy said. "All you have to do is add it up. Like the pastor said, four better, four worse, four richer, four poorer…"

THE PERFECT MISTAKE

My grandfather worked as a carpenter in Chicago, IL, in the 1930s.

On one particular day, he was building some crates for the clothes his church was sending to orphanages in China.

On his way home, he reached into his shirt pocket to find his glasses, but they were gone. When he mentally replayed his earlier actions, he realized what had happened: the glasses had slipped out of his pocket, unnoticed, and fallen into one of the crates, which he had nailed shut. His brand new glasses were heading for China!

The Great Depression was at its height, and Grandpa had six children. He had spent $20 for those glasses that very morning, a considerable amount of money in those days. It was not uncommon for a man to make a dollar a day then. Grandpa was upset by the thought of having to buy another pair.

"It's not fair," he told God as he drove home in frustration. "I've been very faithful in giving of my time and money to your work, and now this."

Months later, the director of the orphanage was on furlough in the United States. He wanted to visit all the churches that supported him in China, so he came to speak one Sunday at my Grandfather's small church in Chicago.

The missionary began by thanking the people for their faithfulness in supporting the orphanage.

"But most of all," he said, "I must thank you for the glasses you sent last year. You see, the Communists had just swept through the orphanage, destroying everything, including my glasses. I was desperate. Even if I had the money, there was simply no way of replacing those glasses. Along with not being able to see well, I experienced headaches every day, so my coworkers and I were much in prayer about this.

"Then your crate arrived. When my staff removed the covers, they found a pair of glasses lying on top." The missionary paused long enough to let his words sink in. Then, still gripped with the wonder of it all, he continued.

"Folks, when I tried on the glasses, it was as though they had been custom-made just for me! I want to thank you for being a part of that."

The people listened, happy for the miraculous glasses. But the missionary surely must have confused their church with another, they thought. There were no glasses on their list of items to be sent overseas.

However, sitting quietly in the back, with tears streaming down his face, an ordinary carpenter realized the Master Carpenter had used him in an extraordinary way. There are times we want to blame God instead of thanking him.

I have to remember this in times of trials.

May God bless your week. Look for the perfect mistakes.

"People are like tea bags—you have to put them in hot water before you know how strong they are." Peace is not the absence of trouble. Peace is the presence of God.

DISCHARGED

Hospital regulations require a wheelchair for patients being discharged. However, while working as a student nurse, I found one elderly gentleman already dressed and sitting on his bed with a suitcase at his feet, who insisted he didn't need my help to leave the hospital.

After a chat about rules being rules, he reluctantly let me wheel him to the elevator.

On the way down, I asked him if his wife was meeting him.

"I don't know," he said. "She's still upstairs in the bathroom changing out of her hospital gown."

A.A.A.D.D.

Recently I was diagnosed with A.A.A.D.D.—Age-Activated Attention Deficit Disorder. This is how it manifests:

I decide to water the garden. As I turn on the hose in the driveway, I look over at my car and decide my car needs washing.

As I start toward the garage, I notice that there is mail on the porch table that I brought up from the mailbox earlier.

I decide to go through the mail before I wash the car. I lay my car keys down on the table, put the junk mail in the garbage can under the table, and notice that the can is full. So I decide to put the bills back on the table and take out the garbage first.

But then I think, since I'm going to be near the mailbox, when I take out the garbage anyway, I may as well pay the bills first. I take my checkbook off the table, and see that there is only one check left. My extra checks are in my desk in the study, so I go inside the house to my desk, where I find the can of Coke that I had been drinking.

I'm going to look for my checks, but first I need to push the Coke aside so that I don't accidentally knock it over. I see that the Coke is getting warm and decide I should put it in the refrigerator to keep it cold.

As I head toward the kitchen with the Coke, a vase

of flowers on the counter catches my eye—they need to be watered.

I set the Coke down on the counter and I discover my reading glasses that I've been searching for all morning. I decide I better put them back on my desk, but first I'm going to water the flowers.

I set the glasses back down on the counter, fill a container with water and suddenly I spot the TV remote. Someone left it on the kitchen table.

I realize that tonight when we go to watch TV, I will be looking for the remote, but I won't remember that it's on the kitchen table. So I decide to put it back in the den where it belongs, but first I'll water the flowers. I pour some water in the flowers, but quite a bit of it spills on the floor. So, I set the remote back down on the table, get some towels, and wipe up the spill.

Then I head down the hall trying to remember what I was planning to do.

At the end of the day:

The car isn't washed,

The bills aren't paid,

There is a warm can of Coke sitting on the counter,

The flowers don't have enough water,

There is still only one check in my checkbook,

I can't find the remote,

I can't find my glasses,

And I don't remember what I did with the car keys.

Then, when I try to figure out why nothing got done

today, I'm really baffled because I know I was busy all day long and I'm really tired.

Growing older is mandatory. Growing up is optional. Laughing at yourself is therapeutic.

P.S. I just remembered I left the water running in the driveway.

TWO WISHES

A man walks into a diner with a full-grown ostrich behind him. The waitress asks them for their orders. The man says, "A hamburger, fries, and a coke," and then turns to the ostrich.

"What's yours?"

"I'll have the same," says the ostrich.

A short time later the waitress returns with the order.

"That will be $9.40 please."

The man reaches into his pocket and pulls out the exact change for payment.

The next day, the man and the ostrich come again and the man says, "A hamburger, fries, and a coke."

The ostrich says, "I'll have the same."

Again the man reaches into his pocket and pays with exact change.

This becomes routine. One day, the two enter again.

"The usual?" asks the waitress.

"No, this is Friday night, so I will have a steak, baked potato, and a salad," says the man.

"Same," says the ostrich.

Shortly the waitress brings the order and says, "That will be $32.62."

Once again the man pulls the exact change out of his pocket and places it on the table.

The waitress cannot hold back her curiosity any longer.

"Excuse me, sir. How do you manage to always come up with the exact change in your pocket every time?"

"Well," says the man, "Several years ago I was cleaning the attic and found an old lamp. When I rubbed it, a genie appeared and offered me two wishes. My first wish was that if I ever had to pay for anything, I would just put my hand in my pocket and the right amount of money would always be there."

"That's brilliant!" says the waitress. "Most people would ask for a million dollars or something, but you'll always be as rich as you want for as long as you live!"

"That's right. Whether it's a gallon of milk or a Rolls Royce, the exact money is always there," says the man.

The waitress asks, "What's with the ostrich?"

The man sighs, pauses and answers.

"My second wish was for a tall chick with a big rear and long legs who agrees with everything I say."

SNIFFER

A man had just settled into his seat next to the window on the plane when another man sat down in the aisle seat and put his black Labrador Retriever in the middle seat next to the man. The first man looked very quizzically at the dog and asked why the dog was allowed on the plane.

The second man explained that he was a DEA agent and that the dog was a "sniffing dog."

"His name is Sniffer and he's the best there is. I'll show you once we get airborne, when I put him to work."

The plane took off, and once it had leveled out, the agent said, "Watch this."

He told Sniffer to "search."

Sniffer jumped down, walked along the aisle, and finally sat very purposefully next to a woman for several seconds. Sniffer then returned to his seat and put one paw on the agent's arm.

The agent said, "Good boy," and turned to the man.

"That woman is in possession of marijuana, so I'm making a note of her seat number and the authorities will apprehend her when we land."

"Say, that's pretty neat," replied the first man.

Once again, the agent sent Sniffer to search the aisles. The lab sniffed, sat down beside a man for a few seconds, returned to its seat, and this time placed two paws on the agent's arm.

The agent said, “That man is carrying cocaine, so again, I’m making a note of his seat number for the police.”

“I like it!” said his seatmate.

The agent then told Sniffer to search again.

Sniffer walked up and down the aisles for a little while, sat down for a moment and then came racing back to the agent. He jumped into the middle seat and proceeded to mess all over the place.

The first man was really grossed out by this behavior and couldn’t figure out how or why a well-trained dog would behave like that, so he asked the agent, “What’s going on?”

The agent nervously replied, “He just found a bomb.”

LEROY/LEIGHROY

A woman walks into the downtown welfare office, trailed by fifteen kids.

"Wow!" the social worker exclaims, "Are they all yours?"

"Yep, they are all mine." The flustered momma sighs, having heard that question a thousand times before.

She says, "Sit down, Leroy."

All the children rush to find seats.

"Well," says the social worker, "Then you must be here to sign up. I'll need your children's names."

"Well, to keep it simple, the boys are all named Leroy and the girls are all named Leighroy."

In disbelief, the caseworker asks, "Are you serious? They're all named Leroy?"

Their momma replied, "Well, yes, it makes it easier. When it's time to get them out of bed and ready for school, I yell, 'Leroy!' And when it's time for dinner, I just yell 'Leroy!' and they all come running. And if I need to stop the kid who's running into the street, I just yell 'Leroy' and all of them stop. It's the smartest idea I ever had, naming 'um all 'Leroy.'"

The social worker thinks this over for a bit, then wrinkles her forehead and says tentatively, "But what if you just want one kid to come, and not the whole bunch?"

"Then I call them by their last names."

THE ARK

In the year 2008, the Lord came unto Noah, who was now living in the United States, and said, "Once again, the earth has become wicked and overpopulated, and I see the end of all flesh before me. Build an ark and save two of every living thing, along with a few good humans."

He gave Noah the blueprints, saying, "You have six months to build the ark before I will start the unending rain for forty days and forty nights."

Six months later, the Lord looked down and saw Noah weeping in his yard—but no ark.

"Noah!" he roared. "I'm about to start the rain! Where is the ark?"

"Forgive me, Lord," begged Noah, "But things have changed. I needed a building permit. I've been arguing with the inspector about the need for a sprinkler system. My neighbors claim that I've violated the neighborhood zoning laws by building the ark in my yard and exceeding the height limitations. We had to go to the Development Appeal Board for a decision.

"Then the Department of Transportation demanded a bond be posted for the future costs of moving power lines and other overhead obstructions, to clear the passage for the Ark's move to the sea. I told them that the sea would be coming to us, but they would hear nothing of it.

"Getting the wood was another problem. There's a ban on cutting local trees in order to save the spotted owl.

I tried to convince the environmentalists that I needed the wood to save the owls, but no go!

"When I started gathering animals, an animal rights group sued me.

"They insisted that I was confining wild animals against their will. They argued the accommodations were too restrictive, and it was cruel and inhumane to put so many animals in a confined space.

"Then the EPA ruled that I couldn't build the ark until they'd conducted an environmental impact study on your proposed flood.

"I'm still trying to resolve a complaint with the Human Rights Commission on how many minorities I'm supposed to hire for my building crew.

"Immigration and Naturalization is checking the green card status of most of the people who want to work.

"The trade unions say I can't use my sons. They insist I have to hire only union workers with ark-building experience.

"To make matters worse, the IRS seized all my assets, claiming I'm trying to leave the country illegally with endangered species.

"So, forgive me, Lord, but it would take at least ten years for me to finish this ark."

Suddenly the skies cleared, the sun began to shine, and a rainbow stretched across the sky.

Noah looked up in wonder and asked, "You mean you're not going to destroy the world?"

"No," said the Lord. "The government beat me to it."

DAFFODILS

Several times my daughter had telephoned to say, "Mother, you must come to see the daffodils before they are over."

I wanted to go, but it was a two-hour drive from Laguna to Lake Arrowhead.

"I will come next Tuesday," I promised a little reluctantly on her third call.

Next Tuesday dawned cold and rainy. Still, I had promised, and reluctantly I drove there. When I finally walked into Carolyn's house, I was welcomed by the joyful sounds of happy children. I delightedly hugged and greeted my grandchildren.

"Forget the daffodils, Carolyn! The road is invisible in these clouds and fog, and there is nothing in the world except you and these children that I want to see badly enough to drive another inch!"

My daughter smiled calmly and said, "We drive in this all the time, Mother."

"Well, you won't get me back on the road until it clears, and then I'm heading for home!" I assured her.

"But first, we're going to see the daffodils. It's just a few blocks," Carolyn said. "I'll drive. I'm used to this."

"Carolyn," I said sternly, "Please turn around."

"It's all right, Mother, I promise. You will never forgive yourself if you miss this experience."

After about twenty minutes, we turned onto a small gravel road and I saw a small church. On the far side of the church, I saw a hand-lettered sign with an arrow that read "Daffodil Garden." We got out of the car, each took a child's hand, and I followed Carolyn down the path. Then, as we turned a corner, I looked up and gasped. Before me lay a most glorious sight. It looked as though someone had taken a great vat of gold and poured it over the mountain and its surrounding slopes. The flowers were planted in majestic, swirling patterns, great ribbons and swaths of deep orange, creamy white, lemon yellow, salmon pink, and saffron and butter yellow.

Each different-colored variety was planted in large groups so that it swirled and flowed like its own river with its own unique hue.

"Who did this?" I asked Carolyn.

"Just one woman," Carolyn answered. "She lives on the property. That's her home." Carolyn pointed to a well-kept A-frame house, small and modestly sitting in the midst of all that glory.

We walked up to the house. On the patio we saw a poster.

"Answers to the Questions I Know You Are Asking," was the headline. The first answer was a simple one.

"50,000 bulbs," it read. The second answer was, "One at a time, by one woman. Two hands, two feet, and one brain."

The third answer was, "Began in 1958."

For me, that moment was a life changing experience. I thought of this woman whom I had never met, who, more than forty years before, had begun, one bulb at a time, to bring her vision of beauty and joy to an obscure mountaintop.

Planting one bulb at a time, year after year, this unknown woman had forever changed the world in which she lived. One day at a time, she had created something of extraordinary magnificence, beauty, and inspiration.

The principle her daffodil garden taught is one of the greatest principles of celebration.

This is learning to move toward our goals and desires one step at a time—often just one baby step at a time—and learning to love the doing, learning to use the accumulation of time.

When we multiply tiny pieces of time with small increments of daily effort, we too will find we can accomplish magnificent things. We can change the world.

"It makes me sad in a way," I admitted to Carolyn. "What might I have accomplished if I had thought of a wonderful goal thirty-five or forty years ago and had worked away at it 'one bulb at a time' through all those years? Just think what I might have been able to achieve!"

My daughter summed up the message of the day in her usual direct way.

"Start tomorrow," she said. She was right. It's so pointless to think of the lost hours of yesterdays. The way to make learning a lesson of celebration instead of a cause for regret is to only ask, "How can I put this to use today?"

Use the Daffodil Principle. Stop waiting…

Until you get a new car or home,

Until your kids leave the house,

Until you go back to school,

Until you finish school,
Until you clean the house,
Until you organize the garage,
Until you clean off your desk,
Until you lose ten lbs.
Until you gain ten lbs.
Until you get married,
Until you have kids,
Until the kids go to school,
Until you retire,
Until summer,
Until spring,
Until winter,
Until fall,
Until you die …

There is no better time than right now to be happy. Happiness is a journey, not a destination. So work like you don't need money. Love like you've never been hurt, and dance like no one is watching. Wishing you a beautiful daffodil day! Don't be afraid that your life will end, be afraid that it will never begin.

LOCAL BAR SUES LOCAL CHURCH

In a small Texas town, a new bar/tavern started a building to open up their business. The local Baptist church started a campaign of petitions and prayers to block the bar from opening.

Work progressed, however, right up till the week before opening, when a lightning strike hit the bar and it burned to the ground.

The church folks were rather smug in their outlook after that, till the bar owner sued the church on the grounds that the church was ultimately responsible for the demise of his building, either through direct or indirect actions or means. The church vehemently denied all responsibility or any connection to the building's demise in its reply to the court.

As the case made its way into court, the judge looked over the paperwork. At the hearing he commented, "I don't know how I'm going to decide this. It appears from the paperwork that we have a bar owner who believes in the power of prayer, and an entire church congregation that doesn't."

PAY FOR THEMSELVES

Last year I replaced all the windows in my house with that expensive double-pane, energy-efficient kind, and today I got a call from the contractor who installed them. He was complaining that the work had been completed a whole year ago and I still hadn't paid for them.

Helllooooo? Just because I'm blonde doesn't mean that I am automatically stupid. So, I told him just what his fast-talking sales guy had told me last year, that in ONE YEAR these windows would pay for themselves!

Well, duh... It's been a year, I told him. There was silence on the other end of the line, so I finally just hung up. He never called back.

We don't stop playing…
Because we grow old…
We grow old…
Because we stop playing…

—George Bernard Shaw

DRINK, STEAL, SWEAR & LIE

I met this guy while I was in Albuquerque and he has a motto he lives by every day. He said listen carefully and live by these four rules: drink, steal, swear, and lie.

I was shaking my head no, but he then told me to listen while he explained his four rules. So here they are:

1. "Drink" from the everlasting cup every day.
2. "Steal" a moment to help someone that is in worse shape than you are.
3. Swear" that you will be a better person today than yesterday.
4. And last, but not least, "lie" down each night, thanking God you live in America and have freedom.

I am not as good as I should be, and I am not as good as I could be. But thank God I am better than I used to be!

EGGS

We went to breakfast at a restaurant where the "senior special" was two eggs, bacon, hash browns, and toast for $1.99.

"Sounds good," my wife said. "But I don't want the eggs."

"Then, I'll have to charge you two dollars and forty nine cents because you're ordering a la carte," the waitress warned her.

"You mean I'd have to pay for not taking the eggs?" my wife said incredulously.

"Yes!" stated the waitress.

"I'll take the special then," my wife said.

"How do you want your eggs?" the waitress asked.

"Raw and in the shell," my wife replied.

She took the two eggs home.

LIFE EXPLAINED

On the first day, God created the dog and said, "Sit all day by the door of your house and bark at anyone who comes in or walks past. For this, I will give you a life span of twenty years."

The dog said, "That's a long time to be barking. How about only ten years and I'll give you back the other ten?"

So God agreed.

On the second day, God created the monkey and said, "Entertain people, do tricks, and make them laugh. For this I'll give you a twenty-year life span."

The monkey said, "Monkey tricks for twenty years? That's a pretty long time to perform. How about I give you back ten like the dog did?"

And God agreed.

On the third day, God created the cow and said, "You must go into the field with the farmer all day long and suffer under the sun, have calves, and give milk to support the farmer's family. For this I will give you a life span of sixty years."

The cow said, "That's kind of a tough life you want me to live for sixty years. How about twenty and I'll give back the other forty?"

And God agreed.

On the fourth day, God created humans and said, "Eat, sleep, play, marry and enjoy your life. For this I'll give you twenty years."

But the human said, "Only twenty years? Could you possibly give me my twenty, the forty the cow gave back, the ten the monkey gave back, and the ten the dog gave back? That makes eighty, okay?"

"Okay," said God, "You asked for it."

So that is why for our first twenty years we eat, sleep, play, and enjoy ourselves. For the next forty years we slave in the sun to support our families. For the next ten years we do monkey tricks to entertain the grandchildren. And for the last ten years we sit on the front porch and bark at everyone.

WHEN THE STORM COMES

Did you know that an eagle knows when a storm is approaching long before it breaks? The eagle will fly to some high spot and wait for the winds to come. When the storm hits, it sets its wings so that the wind will pick it up and lift it above the storm. While the storm rages below, the eagle is soaring above it. The eagle does not escape the storm. It simply uses the storm to lift it higher. It rises on the winds that bring the storm.

When the storms of life come upon us—and all of us will experience them—we can rise above them by setting our minds and our belief toward Jesus.

The storms do not have to overcome us. We can allow God's power to lift us above them. God enables us to ride the winds of the storm that bring sickness, tragedy, failure, and disappointment into our lives. We can soar above the storm.

Remember, it is not the burdens of life that weigh us down; it is how we handle them. The Bible says, "Those who hope in the Lord will renew their strength. They will soar on the wings like eagles" (Isa 40:31).

LOCKED OUT

When my husband and I arrived at an automobile dealership to pick up our car, we were told the keys had been locked in it. We went to the service department and found a mechanic working feverishly to unlock the driver's side door. As I watched from the passenger side, I instinctively tried the door handle and discovered that it was unlocked.

"Hey," I announced to the technician, "it's open."

His reply?

"I know, I already got that side."

BUZZER

The stoplight on the corner buzzes when it's safe to cross the street. I was crossing with an intellectually challenged coworker of mine. She asked if I knew what the buzzer was for. I explained that it signals to blind people when the light is red. Appalled, she responded, "What on earth are blind people doing driving?"

WISDOM

One day I hopped in a taxi and we took off for the airport. We were driving in the right lane when suddenly a black car jumped out of a parking space right in front of us. My taxi driver slammed on his brakes, skidded, and missed the other car by just inches. The driver of the other car whipped his head around and started yelling at us.

My taxi driver just smiled and waved at the guy. And, I mean, he was really friendly.

So I asked, "Why did you just do that? That guy almost ruined your car and sent us to the hospital."

This is when my taxi driver taught me what I now call, "The Law of the Garbage Truck."

He explained that many people are like garbage trucks. They run around full of garbage, frustration, anger, and disappointment. As their garbage piles up, they need a place to dump it, and sometimes they'll dump it on you. Don't take it personally. Just smile, wave, wish them well, and move on. Don't take their garbage and spread it to other people at work, at home, or on the streets.

Life's too short to wake up in the morning with regrets, so love the people who treat you right. Pray for the ones that don't.

GAME WARDEN

One morning the husband returns after several hours of fishing and decides to take a nap. Although not familiar with the lake, the wife decides to take the boat out. She motors out a short distance, anchors, and reads her book.

Along comes a game warden in his boat. He pulls up alongside the woman and says, "Good morning, Ma'am. What are you doing?"

"Reading a book," she replies. (Thinking, "Isn't it obvious?")

"You're in a restricted fishing area," he informs her.

"I'm sorry, officer, but I'm not fishing, I'm reading."

"Yes, but you have all the equipment. For all I know you could start at any moment. I'll have to take you in and write you up."

"If you do that, I'll have to charge you with sexual assault," says the woman.

"But I haven't even touched you," says the game warden.

"That's true, but you have all the equipment. For all I know you could start at any moment."

HIGH-LEVEL BLUNDER:

A large company fired its president after nine months, saying he lacked intellectual leadership. He received a $26 million severance package. Perhaps it's not the president who's lacking intelligence.

WITH A LITTLE HELP FROM OUR FRIENDS:

Police spent two hours attempting to subdue a gunman who had barricaded himself into his home. After firing ten tear gas canisters, officers discovered that the man was standing beside them in the police line, shouting, "Please come out and give yourself up."

WHAT WAS PLAN B?

A man, pretending to have a gun, kidnapped a motorist and forced him to drive to two different automated teller machines, wherein the kidnapper proceeded to withdraw money from his own bank accounts.

THE GETAWAY!

A man walked into a Convenience Store and asked for all the money in the cash drawer. Apparently, the take was too small, so he tied up the store clerk and worked the counter himself for three hours until the police showed up and grabbed him.

DID I SAY THAT?

Police had good luck with a robbery suspect who just couldn't control himself during a lineup. When detectives asked each man in the lineup to repeat the words: "Give me all your money or I'll shoot," the man shouted, "That's not what I said."

ARE WE COMMUNICATING?

A man spoke frantically into the phone.

"My wife is pregnant and her contractions are only two minutes apart."

"Is this her first child?" the doctor asked.

"No," the man shouted, "this is her husband."

NOT THE SHARPEST TOOL IN THE SHED:

A man was arrested for trying to hold up a bank without a weapon. He used a thumb and a finger to simulate a gun. Unfortunately, he failed to keep his hand in his pocket…

THE GRAND FINALE!

Last summer, down on a lake, some folks who were new to boating were having a problem. No matter how hard they tried, they couldn't get their brand-new twenty-two-foot boat going. It was very sluggish in almost every maneuver, no matter how much power they applied. After about an hour of trying to make it go, they putted into a nearby marina, thinking someone there may be able to tell them what was wrong. A thorough topside check revealed everything in perfect working condition. The engine ran fine, the outdrive went up and down, and the propeller was the correct size and pitch. So, one of the marina guys jumped in the water to check underneath. He came up choking on water, he was laughing so hard.

Under the boat, still strapped securely in place, was the trailer!

ADAM'S RIB

At Sunday school, they were teaching how God created everything, including human beings. Little Johnny seemed especially intent when they told him how Eve was created out of one of Adam's ribs.

Later in the week his mother noticed him lying down as though he was ill, and she said, "Johnny, what's the matter?"

Little Johnny responded, "I have a pain in my side. I think I'm going to have a wife."

A COMBINED ENGLISH AND MATH TEST FOR YOUR GRANDCHILDREN:

1. What is one and one?
2. What is the sum of one plus one?

Answers:

1. Eleven.
2. Two.

LOST WIVES

Two guys, one old and one young, are pushing their carts around Home Depot when they collide.

The old guy says to the young guy, "Sorry about that. I'm looking for my wife, and I guess I wasn't paying attention to where I was going."

The young guy says, "That's okay. It's a coincidence. I'm looking for my wife too. I can't find her, and I'm getting a little desperate."

The old guy says, "Maybe we can help each other. What does your wife look like?"

The young guy says, "Well, she's twenty-four years old, tall, with blonde hair, blue eyes, long legs, big bust, and she's wearing tight white shorts, a halter top, and no bra. What does your wife look like?"

The old guy says, "Doesn't matter. Let's look for yours."

TRICKY BOB

A man is getting into the shower just as his wife is finishing up her shower, when the doorbell rings. The wife quickly wraps herself in a towel and runs downstairs. When she opens the door, there stands Bob, the next-door neighbor.

Before she says a word, Bob says, "I'll give you $800 to drop that towel."

After thinking for a moment, the woman drops her towel and stands there in front of Bob.

After a few seconds, Bob hands her $800 and leaves.

The woman wraps back up in the towel and goes back upstairs. When she gets to the bathroom, her husband asks, "Who was that?"

"It was Bob, the next door neighbor," she replies.

"Great," the husband says. "Did he say anything about the $800 he owes me?"

DIDDIES

Elsewhere, a carjacker in Los Angeles stole a tank of gas but left the Mercedes.

Where does the one-legged waitress work?
At IHOP.

What do you call a boomerang that doesn't come back?
A stick!

Spouse: Someone who'll stand by you through all the trouble you wouldn't have had if you'd stayed single.

Question: Where is the most dangerous traffic area in the United States?
Answer: Your local church parking lot immediately after the conclusion of Sunday services.

Old is when you're not sure these are jokes.

THE OLD PATHS

I like the old paths
When moms were at home
Dads were at work
Brothers went into the Army
And sisters got married *before* having children.

Crime did not pay;
Hard work did;
And people knew the difference.

Moms could cook;
Dads would work;
Children would behave ...

Husbands were loving;
Wives were supportive;
And children were polite.

Women wore the jewelry;
And men wore the pants.
Women looked like ladies;
Men looked like gentlemen;
And children looked decent.

People loved the truth,
And hated a lie;
They came to church to get *in*,
Not to get *out!*

Hymns sounded godly;
Sermons sounded helpful;
Rejoicing sounded normal;
And crying sounded sincere.

Cursing was wicked;
Drinking was evil;
And divorce was unthinkable.

The flag was honored;
America was beautiful
And God was welcome!

We read the Bible in public;

Prayed in school;
And preached from house to house
To be called an American was worth dying for;
To be called a Christian was worth living for;
To be called a traitor was a shame!

Sex was a personal word.
Homosexual was an unheard of word,
And abortion was an illegal word.

Preachers preached because they had a message;
And Christians rejoiced because they had the *victory!*
Preachers preached from the Bible;
Singers sang from the heart;
And sinners turned to the Lord to be *saved!*

A new birth meant a new life;
Salvation meant a changed life;
Following Christ led to eternal life.

Being a preacher meant
you proclaimed the word of God;
Being a deacon meant you would serve the Lord;
Being a Christian meant you would live for Jesus;
And being a sinner meant someone was praying for you!

Laws were based on the Bible;
Homes read the Bible;
And churches taught the Bible.

Preachers were more interested in new converts
Than new clothes and new cars.
God was worshiped;
Christ was exalted;
And the Holy Spirit was respected.

Church was where you found Christians
On the Lord's day, rather than in the garden,
On the creek bank, on the golf course,
Or being entertained somewhere else.

I still like the old paths the best!

WOMAN'S PERFECT BREAKFAST

She's sitting at the table with her gourmet coffee.
Her son is on the cover of the Wheaties box.
Her daughter is on the cover of *Business Week.*
Her boyfriend is on the cover of *Playgirl.*
And her husband is on the back of the milk carton.

WOMEN'S REVENGE

"Cash, check, or charge?" I asked, after folding items the woman wished to purchase.

As she fumbled for her wallet, I noticed a remote control for a television set in her purse.

"So, do you always carry your TV remote?" I asked.

"No," she replied, "but my husband refuses to come shopping with me, and I figured this was the most evil thing I could do to him legally."

UNDERSTANDING WOMEN

(A Man's Perspective)

I know I'm not going to understand women.
I'll never understand how you can take boiling hot wax,
Pour it onto your upper thigh; rip the hair out by the root,
And still be afraid of a spider.

MARRIAGE SEMINAR

While attending a marriage seminar dealing with communication,

Tom and his wife Grace listened to the instructor.

"It's essential that husbands and wives know each other's likes and dislikes."

He addressed the man, "Can you name your wife's favorite flower?"

Tom leaned over, touched his wife's arm gently and whispered, "It's Pillsbury, isn't it?"

WIFE VS. HUSBAND

A couple drove down a country road for several miles, not saying a word.

An earlier discussion had led to an argument and neither of them wanted to concede their position.

As they past a barnyard of mules, goats, and pigs, the husband asked sarcastically, “Relatives of yours?”

“Yep,” the wife replied, “In-laws.”

WHO DOES WHAT

A man and his wife were having an argument about who should brew the coffee each morning.

The wife said, "You should do it because you get up first, and then we don't have to wait as long to get our coffee.

The husband said, "You are in charge of cooking around here and you should do it, because that is your job, and I can just wait for my coffee."

Wife replies, "No, you should do it, and besides, it is in the Bible that the man should do the coffee."

Husband replies, "I can't believe that, show me." So she fetched the Bible, opened the New Testament, and showed him at the top of several pages that it indeed says "*Hebrews.*"

THE SILENT TREATMENT

A man and his wife were having some problems at home, and were giving each other the silent treatment. Suddenly, the man realized that the next day, he would need his wife to wake him at 5:00am for an early morning business flight. Not wanting to be the first to break the silence (and *lose*), he wrote on a piece of paper, "Please wake me at 5:00 a.m." He left it where he knew she would find it. The next morning, the man woke up, only to discover it was 9:00am and he had missed his flight. Furious, he was about to go and see why his wife hadn't wakened him, when he noticed a piece of paper by the bed. The paper said, "It is 5:00am. Wake up."

PRESCRIPTION

A distraught senior citizen phoned her doctor's office.

"Is it true," she wanted to know, "that the medication you prescribed has to be taken for the rest of my life?"

"Yes, I'm afraid so," the doctor told her.

There was a moment of silence before the senior lady replied,

"I'm wondering then, just how serious is my condition? Because this prescription is marked '*no refills.*'"

DO YOUR BEST

An older gentleman was on the operating table awaiting surgery, and he insisted that his son, a renowned surgeon, perform the operation. As he was about to get the anesthesia, he asked to speak to his son.

"Yes, Dad, what is it?"

"Don't be nervous, son; do your best and just remember, if it doesn't go well, if something happens to me, your mother is going to come and live with you and your wife."

AGING

Eventually you will reach a point
When you stop lying about your age
And start bragging about it.

The older we get,
The fewer things
Seem worth waiting in line for.

When you are dissatisfied
And would like to go back to youth,
Think of algebra.

First you forget names,
Then you forget faces.
Then you forget to pull up your zipper.
It's worse when you forget to pull it down.

SPEEDER

Billy Graham was returning to Charlotte after a speaking engagement, and when his plane arrived, there was a limousine there to transport him to his home. As he prepared to get into the limo, he stopped and spoke to the driver.

"You know," he said, "I am eighty-seven years old and I have never driven a limousine. Would you mind if I drove it for a while?"

The driver said, "No problem, have at it."

Billy gets into the driver's seat and they head off down the highway. A short distance away sat a rookie State Trooper operating his first speed trap. The long black limo went by him doing 70 in a 55 mph zone. The trooper pulled out and easily caught the limo and he got out of his patrol car to begin the procedure. The young trooper walked up to the driver's door, and when the glass was rolled down, he was surprised to see who was driving. He immediately excused himself and went back to his car and called his supervisor.

He told the supervisor, "I know we are supposed to enforce the law, but I also know that important people are given certain courtesies. I need to know what I should do because I have stopped a very important person."

The supervisor asked, "Is it the governor?"

The young trooper said, "No, he's more important than that."

The supervisor said, "Oh, so it's the president."

The young trooper said, "No, he's even more important than that."

The supervisor finally asked, "Well then, who is it?"

The young trooper said, "I think it's Jesus, because he's got Billy Graham for a chauffeur."

THE NOTE

The children were lined up in the cafeteria of a Catholic elementary school for lunch. At the head of the table was a large pile of apples. The nun made a note, and posted it on the apple tray:

"Take only *one*—God is watching."

Moving further along the lunch line, at the other end of the table was a large pile of chocolate chip cookies.

A child had written a note, "Take all you want. God is watching the apples."

DANCING

Imagine you and the Lord Jesus are walking down a dirt road together. For much of the way, the Lord's footprints go along steadily, consistently, rarely varying the pace.

But your footprints are a disorganized stream of zigzags, starts, stops, turnarounds, circles, departures, and returns.

For much of the way, it seems to go like this, but gradually your footprints come more in line with the Lord's, soon paralleling his consistently.

You and Jesus are walking as true friends!

This seems perfect, but then an interesting thing happens: Your footprints that once etched the sand next to Jesus' are now walking precisely in his step.

Inside his larger footprints are your smaller ones. You and Jesus are becoming one.

This goes on for many miles, but gradually you notice another change. The footprints inside the large footprints seem to grow larger.

Eventually they disappear altogether. There is only one set of footprints. They have become one.

This goes on for a long time, but suddenly the second set of footprints is back. This time it seems even worse. Zigzags all over the place. Stops. Starts. Gashes in the sand. A variable mess of prints.

You are amazed and shocked. Your dream ends. Now you pray:

"Lord, I understand the first scene, with zigzags and fits. I was a new Christian; I was just learning. But you walked on through the storm and helped me learn to walk with you."

"That is correct."

"And when the smaller footprints were inside of yours, I was actually learning to walk in your steps, following you very closely."

"Very good . . . you have understood everything so far."

"When the smaller footsteps grew and filled in yours, I supposed that I was becoming like you in every way."

"Precisely."

"So, Lord, was there a regression or something? The footprints separated, and this time it was worse than at first."

There is a pause as the Lord answers, with a smile in his voice.

"You didn't know? It was then that we danced."

"To everything there is a season, a time for every purpose under Heaven: A time to weep, a time to laugh, a time to mourn, and a time to dance" (Ecclesiastes 3:1).

BUBBA

Bubba goes to the revival and listens to the preacher. After a while, the preacher asks anyone with needs to come forward and be prayed over. Bubba gets in line.

When it's his turn the preacher says, "Bubba, what do you want me to pray about?"

Bubba says, "Preacher, I need you to pray for my hearing."

So the preacher puts one finger in Bubba's ear and the other hand on top of his head and prays a while. After a few minutes he removes his hands and says, "Bubba, how's your hearing now?"

Bubba says, "I don't know, preacher, it's not until next Wednesday at the courthouse."

MOM OVER FOR DINNER

(you don't even have to be a mother to enjoy this one)

Brian invited his mother over for dinner. During the course of the meal, Brian's mother couldn't help but notice how beautiful Brian's roommate, Jennifer, was. Brian's mom had long been suspicious of a relationship between Brian and Jennifer, and this had only made her more curious.

Over the course of the evening, while watching the two interact, she started to wonder if there was more between Brian and Jennifer than met the eye.

Reading his mom's thoughts, Brian volunteered, "I know what you must be thinking, but I assure you Jennifer and I are just roommates."

About a week later, Jennifer came to Brian, saying, "Ever since your mother came to dinner, I've been unable to find the beautiful silver gravy ladle. You don't suppose she took it, do you?"

Brian said, "Well, I doubt it, but I'll send her an e-mail just to be sure." So he sat down and wrote:

Dear Mom:

I'm not saying that you 'did' take the gravy ladle from the house, and I'm not saying that you 'did not' take the gravy ladle. But the fact remains that one has been missing ever since you were here for dinner.

Love, Brian

Several days later, Brian received an e-mail back from his mother that read:

Dear Son,

I'm not saying that you 'do' sleep with Jennifer. I'm not saying that you 'do not' sleep with Jennifer. But the fact remains that if Jennifer were sleeping in her own bed, she would have found the gravy ladle by now.

Love, Mom

WOMAN'S INTELLIGENCE

Two men were standing at the base of a flagpole looking up. A woman walked by and asked what they were doing.

"We're supposed to find the height of the flagpole," one man said, "but we don't have a ladder."

The woman took a wrench from her purse, loosened a few bolts, and laid the pole down.

Then she took a tape measure from her pocketbook, took a measurement, announced, "Eighteen feet, six inches," and walked away.

The men shook their heads and laughed.

"Ain't that just like a woman? We ask for the height and she gives us the length."

THE BEAR AND THE ATHEIST

An atheist was walking through the woods.

"What majestic trees! What powerful rivers! What beautiful animals," he said to himself.

As he was walking alongside the river, he heard a rustling in the bushes behind him.

He turned to look. He saw a seven-foot grizzly bear charge towards him. He ran as fast as he could up the path. He looked over his shoulder and saw that the bear was closing in on him.

He looked over his shoulder again, and the bear was even closer. He tripped and fell to the ground.

He rolled over to pick himself up but saw that the bear was right on top of him, reaching for him with his left paw, and raising his right paw to strike him.

At that instant the atheist cried out, "*Oh my God!*"

Time stopped. The bear froze. The forest was silent.

As a bright light shone upon the man, a voice came out of the sky.

"You deny my existence for all these years, teach others that I don't exist, and even credit creation to cosmic accident. Do you expect me to help you out of this predicament? Am I to count you as a believer?

The atheist looked directly into the light.

"It would be hypocritical of me to suddenly ask you to treat me as a Christian now, but perhaps you could make the *bear* a Christian."

"Very well," said the voice.

The light went out. The sounds of the forest resumed. The bear dropped his right paw, brought both paws together, bowed his head and spoke.

"Lord, bless this food, which I am about to receive from thy bounty through Christ our Lord, Amen."

CURSING PARROT

So, there's this guy with a parrot. And this parrot swears like a sailor. I mean he's a pistol. He can swear for five minutes straight without repeating himself. Trouble is, the guy who owns him is a quiet, conservative type, and this bird's foul mouth is driving him crazy.

One day, it gets to be too much. The guy grabs the bird by the throat, shakes him really hard, and yells, "*Quit it!*"

But this just makes the bird mad and he swears more than ever.

Then the guy gets mad and says, "Ok, for you . . ."

He locks the bird in a kitchen cabinet. This really aggravates the bird, and he claws and scratches. When the guy finally lets him out, the bird cuts loose with a stream of vulgarities that would make a veteran sailor blush.

At this point, the guy is so mad that he throws the bird into the freezer. For the first few seconds, the bird kicks and claws and thrashes. Then it suddenly gets very, very quiet.

At first, the guy just waits, but then he starts to think that the bird may be hurt. After a couple of minutes of silence, he's so worried that he opens up the freezer door.

The bird calmly climbs onto the man's outstretched arm and says: "Awfully sorry about the trouble I gave you. I'll do my best to improve my vocabulary from now on."

The man is astounded. He can't understand the transformation that has come over the parrot.

Then the parrot says, "By the way, what did the chicken in the freezer do?"

LIVING WILL

Last night, my husband and I were sitting in the living room and I said to him, "I never want to live in a vegetative state, dependent on some machine or fluids from a bottle. If that ever happens, just pull the plug."

He got up, unplugged the computer, and threw out my Diet Coke.

FOUR YEAR OLD

A four-year-old child's next-door neighbor was an elderly gentleman who had recently lost his wife. Upon seeing the man cry, the little boy went into the old gentleman's yard, climbed on to his lap, and just sat there. When his mother asked him what he had said to the neighbor, the little boy just said, "Nothing, I just helped him cry."

FIRST GRADERS

Some first graders were discussing a picture of a family. One little boy in the picture had a different hair color than the other members. One of her students suggested that he was adopted. A little girl said, "I know all about adoption, I was adopted."

"What does it mean to be adopted?" asked another child.

"It means," said the girl, "that you grew in your mommy's heart instead of her tummy."

LITTLE LEAGUE

On my way home one day, I stopped to watch a Little League baseball game that was being played in a park near my home. As I sat down behind the bench on the first base line, I asked one of the boys what the score was.

"We're behind 14 to nothing," he answered with a smile.

"Really," I said. "I have to say you don't look very discouraged."

"Discouraged?" the boy asked with a puzzled look on his face. "Why should we be discouraged? We haven't been up to bat yet."

CHOSEN

Whenever I'm disappointed with my spot in life, I stop and think about little Jamie Scott. Jamie was trying out for a part in the school play. His mother told me that he's set his heart on being in it, though she feared he would not be chosen.

On the day the parts were awarded, I went with her to collect him after school. Jamie rushed up to her, eyes shining with pride and excitement.

"Guess what, Mom," he shouted, and then said words that will remain a lesson to me. "I've been chosen to clap and cheer."

SHOES AND SOCKS

On a cold day in December, some years ago, a little boy about ten years old, was standing before a shoe store. He was barefoot, peering through the window, and shivering with cold.

A lady approached the young boy and said, "My, but you're in such deep thought staring in that window!"

"I was asking God to give me a pair of shoes," was the boy's reply.

The lady took him by the hand, went into the store, and asked the clerk to get half a dozen pairs of socks for the boy. She then asked if he could give her a basin of water and a towel. He quickly brought them to her. She took the little fellow to the back part of the store, and, removing her gloves, knelt down, washed his little feet, and dried them with a towel.

By this time, the clerk had returned with the socks. Placing a pair upon the boy's feet, she then proceeded to purchase him a pair of shoes.

She tied up the remaining pair of socks and gave them to him. She patted him on the head and said, "No doubt, you will be more comfortable now."

As she turned to go, the astonished kid caught her by the hand, and looking up into her face, with tears in his eyes, asked her, "Are you God's wife?"

LIFE AFTER DEATH

"Do you believe in life after death?" the boss asked one of his employees.

"Yes, sir," the new employee replied.

"Well then, that makes everything just fine," the boss went on. "After you left early yesterday to go to your grandmother's funeral, she stopped in to see you."

PALM SUNDAY

It was Palm Sunday, and because of a sore throat, five-year-old Johnny stayed home from church with a sitter. When the family returned home, they were carrying several palm branches. The boy asked what they were for.

"People held them over Jesus' head as he walked by."

"Wouldn't you know it," the boy fumed. "The only Sunday I don't go, He shows up!"

CHILDREN'S SERMON

One Easter Sunday morning as the minister was preaching the children's sermon, he reached into his bag of props and pulled out an egg. He pointed at the egg and asked the children, "What's in here?"

"I know!" a little boy exclaimed. "Pantyhose."

SUPPORT A FAMILY

The prospective father in-law asked, “Young man, can you support a family?”

The surprised groom-to-be replied, “Well, no. I was just planning to support your daughter. The rest of you will have to fend for yourselves.”

PRAYERS

The Sunday school teacher asked, "Now, Johnny, tell me, do you say prayers before eating?"

"No, sir," he replied. "We don't have to. My Mom is a good cook!"

CLIMB THE WALLS

"Oh, I sure am happy to see you," the little boy said to his grandmother on his mother's side. "Now maybe Daddy will do the trick he has been promising us."

The grandmother was curious.

"What trick is that?" she asked.

"I heard him tell Mommy that he would climb the walls if you came to visit," the little boy answered.

THE MOOD RING

My husband bought me a mood ring the other day. When I'm in a good mood it turns green. When I'm in a bad mood, it leaves a red mark on his forehead.

THE WATER PISTOL

When my three-year-old son opened the birthday gift from his grandmother, he discovered a water pistol. He squealed with delight and headed for the nearest sink.

I was not so pleased. I turned to Mom and said, "I'm surprised at you. Don't you remember how we used to drive you crazy with water guns?"

Mom smiled and then replied, "I remember!"

NEW TEACHER

A new teacher was trying to make use of her psychology courses. She started her class by saying, "Everyone who thinks they're stupid, stand up!"

After a few seconds, Little Davie stood up. The teacher said, "Do you think you're stupid, Little Davie?"

"No, ma'am, but I hate to see you standing there all by yourself."

COLD CREAM

Little Davie watched, fascinated, as his mother smoothed cold cream on her face.

"Why do you do that, mommy?" he asked.

"To make myself beautiful," said his mother, who then began removing the cream with a tissue.

"What's the matter?" asked Little Davie. "Giving up?"

GRANDMA'S AGE

Little Johnny asked his grandma how old she was.

Grandma answered, "39 and holding."

Johnny thought for a moment, and then said, "And how old would you be if you let go?"

PUMPKIN

A woman was asked by a coworker, “What is it like to be a Christian?”

The coworker replied, “It is like being a pumpkin. God picks you from the patch, brings you in, and washes all the dirt off of you. Then he cuts off the top and scoops out all the yucky stuff. He removes the seeds of doubt, hate, and greed. Then he carves you a new smiling face and puts His light inside of you to shine for all the world to see.”

SIGNS

Sign over a gynecologist's office:
Dr. Jones, at your cervix.

In a podiatrist's office:
Time wounds all heels.

On a septic tank truck:
Yesterday's meals on wheels.

At a proctologist's door:
To expedite your visit, please back in.

On a plumber's truck:
We repair what your husband fixed.

On another plumber's truck:
Don't sleep with a drip; call your plumber!

On a church's billboard:
Seven days without God makes one weak.

At a tire shop:
Invite us to your next blowout…

At a towing company:
We don't charge you an arm and a leg: we want tows.

On an electrician's truck:
Let us remove your shorts.

In a non-smoking area:
If we see smoke, we will assume you are on fire and take appropriate action.

On a maternity room door:
Push. Push. Push!!!

At an optometrist's office:
If you don't see what you're looking for, you've come to the right place.

On a taxidermist's window:
We really know our stuff.

Sign on a fence:
Salesmen welcome! Dog food is expensive …

At a car dealership:
The best way to get back on your feet; miss a car payment.

Outside a muffler shop:
No appointment necessary; we hear you coming.

In a veterinarian's waiting room:
Be back in 5 minutes—sit, stay!

At the electric company:
We will be de-lighted if you send in your payment.

However, if you don't, you will be.

In a restaurant window:
Don't stand there and be hungry; come on in and get fed up.

In the front yard of a funeral home:
Drive carefully! We'll wait …

At a propane filling station:
Thank heaven for little grills.

THE DENTURES

The minister just had all of his remaining teeth pulled and new dentures were being made.

The first Sunday, he only preached ten minutes. The second Sunday, he preached only twenty minutes. But, on the third Sunday, he preached one hour and twenty-five minutes.

When asked about this by some of the congregation, he responded this way:

"The first Sunday, my gums were so sore it hurt to talk. The second Sunday, my new dentures were hurting me a lot. The third Sunday, I accidentally grabbed my wife's dentures … and I couldn't shut up."

POLISH DIVORCE

A Polish man moved to the USA and married an American girl. Although his English was far from perfect, they got along very well. One day he rushed into a lawyer's office and asked him if he could arrange a divorce for him. The lawyer said that getting a divorce would depend on the circumstances, and asked him the following questions:

Have you any grounds?

Yes, an acre and a half and a nice little home.

No, I mean what is the foundation of this case?

It's made of concrete.

I don't think you understand. Do either of you have a real grudge?

No, we have a carport, and no need for one.

I mean, what is your relationship like?

All my relations are still in Poland.

Is there any infidelity in your marriage?

We have a hi-fidelity stereo and a good DVD player.

Does your wife beat you up?

No, I am always up before her.

Why do you want this divorce?

She's going to kill me.

What makes you think that?

I got proof.

What kind of proof?

She's going to poison me. She bought a bottle at the drugstore and put it on a shelf in the bathroom. I can read, and it says: "*Polish remover.*"

PUZZLED FATHER

Su Wong marries Lee Wong. The next year, the Wongs have a new baby. The nurse brings over a lovely, healthy, bouncy, but definitely Caucasian, white baby boy.

"Congratulations," says the nurse to the new parents. "Well, Mr. Wong, what will you and Mrs. Wong name the baby?"

The puzzled father looks at his new baby boy and says, "Well, two Wongs don't make a white, so I think we will name him …"

Are you ready for this?

Sum Ting Wong

VIRGIL

"Hello, is this the Sheriff's Office?"

"Yes. What can I do for you?"

"I'm calling to report 'bout my neighbor Virgil. He's hidin' marijuana inside his firewood! Don't quite know how he gets it inside them logs, but he's hidin' it there."

"Thank you very much for the call, sir."

The next day, twelve sheriff's deputies descend on Virgil's house. They search the shed where the firewood is kept. Using axes, they bust open every piece of wood, but find no marijuana. They sneer at Virgil and leave.

Shortly, the phone rings at Virgil's house.

"Hey, Virgil! This here's Floyd... did the sheriff come?"

"Yeah."

"Did they chop your firewood?"

"Yep!"

"Happy Birthday, buddy!"

"GOODBYE MOM!"

A young man shopping in a supermarket noticed a little old lady following him around. If he stopped, she stopped. Furthermore, she kept staring at him.

She finally overtook him at the checkout, and she turned to him and said, "I hope I haven't made you feel ill at ease; it's just that you look so much like my late son."

He answered, "That's okay."

"I know it's silly, but if you'd call out, 'Goodbye, Mom' as I leave the store, it would make me feel so happy."

She then went through the checkout, and as she was on her way out of the store, the man called out, "Goodbye, Mom."

The little old lady waved and smiled back at him.

Pleased that he had brought a little sunshine into someone's day, he went to pay for his groceries.

"That comes to $121.85," said the clerk.

"How come so much? I only bought five items ..."

The clerk replied, "Yeah, but your mother said you'd be paying for her things, too."

ELBOWS

An Italian grandmother is giving directions to her grown grandson, who is coming to visit with his wife.

"You comma to de front door of the apartmenta. I am inna apartmenta 301. There issa bigga panel at the front door. With your elbow, pusha button 301. I will buzza you in. Come inside, the elevator is on the right. Get in, and with you elbow, pusha three. When you get out, I'mma on the left. With your elbow, hit my doorbell."

"Grandma, that sounds easy, but why am I hitting all these buttons with my elbow?"

"What... you coming empty-handed?"

OFFERINGS

This may come as a surprise to those of you not living in Las Vegas, but there are more Catholic churches than casinos.

Not surprisingly, some worshipers at Sunday services will give casino chips rather than cash when the basket is passed.

Since they get chips from many different casinos, the churches have devised a method to collect the offerings.

The churches send all their collected chips to a nearby Franciscan monastery for sorting and then the chips are taken to the casinos of origin and cashed in.

This is done by the Chip Monks.

WISHES

A sales rep, an administrative clerk, and the manager are walking to lunch when they find an antique oil lamp. They rub it and a genie comes out. The genie says, "I'll give each of you just one wish."

"Me first! Me first!" says the administrative clerk. "I want to be in the Bahamas, driving a speedboat, without a care in the world."

Poof! She's gone.

"Me next! Me next!" says the sales rep. "I want to be in Hawaii, relaxing on the beach with my personal masseuse, an endless supply of Pina Coladas, and the love of my life."

Poof! He's gone.

"Ok, you're up," the genie says to the manager.

The manager says, "I want those two back in the office after lunch."

WINTER BLONDE

As a trucker stops for a red light, a blonde catches up. She jumps out of her car, runs up to his truck, and knocks on the door. The trucker lowers the window, and she says, "Hi, my name is Heather, and you're losing some of your load."

The trucker ignores her and proceeds down the street. When the truck stops for another red light, the girl catches up again. She jumps out of her car, runs up, and knocks on the door. Again the trucker lowers the window. As if they've never spoken, the blonde says brightly, "Hi, my name is Heather, and you are losing some of your load."

Shaking his head, the trucker ignores her again and continues down the street. At the third red light, the same thing happens. All out of breath, the blonde gets out of her car, runs up, and knocks on the truck door. The trucker rolls down the window. Again she says, "Hi, my name is Heather, and you are losing some of your load!"

When the light turns green the trucker revs up and races to the next light. When he stops this time, he hurriedly gets out of the truck, and runs back to the blonde.

He knocks on her window, and after she lowers it, he says, "Hi, my name is Kevin. It's winter, it's snowing, and I'm driving the *salt truck!*"

"IT PAYS TO TELL THE TRUTH"

Jack decided to go skiing with his buddy, Bob. They loaded up Jack's minivan and headed north. After driving for a few hours, they got caught in a terrible blizzard. They pulled into a nearby farm and asked the attractive lady who answered the door if they could spend the night.

"I realize it's terrible weather out there and I have this huge house all to myself, but I'm recently widowed," she explained. "I'm afraid the neighbors will talk if I let you stay in my house."

"Don't worry," Jack said. "We'll be happy to sleep in the barn. And if the weather breaks, we'll be gone at first light."

The lady agreed, and the two men found their way to the barn and settled in for the night. Come morning, the weather had cleared, and they got on their way. They enjoyed a great weekend of skiing. About nine months later, Jack got an unexpected letter from an attorney.

It took him a few minutes to figure it out, but he finally determined that it was from the attorney of that attractive widow he had met on the ski weekend. He dropped in on his friend Bob and asked, "Bob, do you remember that good-looking widow from the farm we stayed at on our ski holiday up north?"

"Yes, I do," said Bob.

"Did you happen to get up in the middle of the night, go up to the house, and pay her a visit?"

"Yes," Bob said, a little embarrassed about being found out. "I have to admit that I did."

"And did you happen to use my name instead of telling your name?"

Bob's face turned red and he said, "Yeah, sorry, buddy. I'm afraid I did. Why do you ask?"

"She just died and left me everything."

BUY A CAT

If you want someone who will bring you the paper without first tearing it apart to remove the sports section—then buy a dog.

If you want someone willing to make a fool of himself simply over the joy of seeing you—then buy a dog.

If you want someone who will eat whatever you put in front of him and never says it's not quite as good as his mother made it—then buy a dog.

If you want someone always willing to go out, at any hour, for as long and wherever you want—then buy a dog.

If you want someone who will never touch the remote, doesn't care about football, and can sit next to you as you watch romantic movies—then buy a dog.

If you want someone who is content to get up on your bed just to warm your feet and whom you can push off if he snores—then buy a dog.

If you want someone who never criticizes what you do, doesn't care if you are pretty or ugly, fat or thin, young or old, who acts as if every word you say is especially worthy of listening to, and loves you unconditionally, perpetually—then buy a dog.

But on the other hand, if you want someone who will never come when you call, ignores you totally when you come home, leaves hair all over the place, walks all over you, runs around all night and only comes home to eat and sleep, and acts as if your entire existence is solely to ensure his happiness—then buy a *cat!*

INTERESTING STORIES

1. I am a medical student currently doing a rotation in toxicology at the poison control center. Today, this woman called in very upset because she caught her little daughter eating ants. I quickly reassured her that the ants are not harmful and there would be no need to bring her daughter in to the hospital. She calmed down and at the end of the conversation happened to mention that she gave her daughter some ant poison to eat in order to kill the ants. I told her she had better bring her daughter into the emergency room right away.

2. Some employees on an airfield decided to steal a life raft from one of the larger aircraft. They were successful in getting it out of the plane and home. Shortly after, they took it for a float on the river. They noticed a Coast Guard helicopter coming towards them. It turned out that the chopper was homing in on the emergency locator beacon that activated when the raft was inflated. They are no longer employed.

3. A man, wanting to rob a downtown bank, walked into a branch and wrote this: "Put all your money in this bag." While standing in line waiting to give his note to the teller, he began to worry someone had seen him write the note and might call the police before he reached the teller's window.

So he left the bank and crossed the street to another bank. After waiting a few minutes in line, he handed his note to the bank teller. She read it and, surmising from his spelling errors that he wasn't the brightest light in the harbor, told him that she could not accept his stickup note because it was written on another bank's deposit slip. He would either have to fill out a new deposit slip or go back to the other bank. Looking somewhat defeated, the man said, "Okay," and left. He was arrested a few minutes later as he was waiting in line back at the original bank.

4. A motorist was unknowingly caught in an automated speed trap that measured his speed using radar and photographed his car. He later received in the mail a ticket for forty dollars and a photo of his car. Instead of payment, he sent the police department a photo of forty dollars. Several days later, he received a letter from the police that contained another picture, this time it was of handcuffs. He immediately mailed in his forty dollars.

5. A guy walked into a little corner store with a shotgun and demanded all of the cash from the cash drawer. After the cashier put the cash in a bag, the robber saw a bottle of scotch that he wanted behind the counter on the shelf. He told the cashier to put it in the bag as well, but the cashier refused and said, "I don't believe you are over twenty-one."

The robber said he was, but the clerk still refused to give it to him because she didn't believe him.

At this point, the robber took his driver's license out of his wallet and gave it to the clerk. The clerk looked it over and agreed that the man was in fact over twenty-one. She put the Scotch in the bag.

The robber then ran from the store with his loot. The cashier promptly called the police and gave the name and address of the robber that she got off the license. They arrested the robber two hours later.

6. A pair of robbers entered a record shop, nervously waving revolvers. The first one shouted, "Nobody move!" When his partner moved, the startled first bandit shot him.

7. Seems this guy wanted some beer pretty badly. He decided that he'd just throw a cinder block through a liquor store window, grab some booze, and run. So he lifted the cinder block and heaved it over his head at the window. The cinder block bounced back, knocking him unconscious. It seems the liquor store window was made of Plexiglass. The whole event was caught on videotape.

8. *In the Neighborhood:* I live in a semi-rural area. We recently had a new neighbor call the local township administrative office to request the removal of the "deer crossing" sign on our road. The reason: "Too many deer are being hit by cars out here! I don't think this is a good place for them to be crossing anymore."

9. *Fast Food Service:* My daughter went to a local taco restaurant and ordered a taco. She asked the person

behind the counter for "minimal lettuce." He said he was sorry but they only had iceberg.

10. *Sighting:* I was at the airport, checking in at the gate when an airport employee asked, "Has anyone put anything in your baggage without your knowledge?" To which I replied, "If it was without my knowledge, how would I know?" He smiled knowingly and nodded, "That's why we ask."

11. *Sighting:* At a goodbye luncheon for an old and dear co-worker who was leaving the company due to "downsizing," our manager commented cheerfully, "This is fun. We should do this more often." Not another word was spoken. We all just looked at each other with that deer-in-the-headlights stare.

12. *Sighting:* I work with an individual who plugged her power strip back into itself and for the sake of her own life, couldn't understand why her system would not turn on.

GAMES FOR WHEN WE ARE OLDER:

1. Sag, you're it
2. Hide and go wee
3. Twenty Questions shouted into your good ear
4. Kick the bucket
5. Red Rover, Red Rover, the nurse says bend over
6. Musical recliners
7. Simon says something incoherent
8. Pin the toupee on the bald guy

SIGNS OF MENOPAUSE:

1. You sell your house heating system at a yard sale
2. You have to write post-it notes with your kids' names on them
3. You change your underwear after a sneeze

OLD IS WHEN:

1. Going bra-less pulls all the wrinkles out of your face
2. You don't care where your spouse goes, just as long as you don't have to go along
3. Getting a little action means you don't need fiber today
4. Getting lucky means you find your car in the parking lot
5. An all-nighter means not getting up to wee!

CUTE THOUGHTS

Wouldn't it be nice if whenever we messed up our life we could simply press "Ctrl, Alt, Del" and start all over?

If raising children was going to be easy, it never would have started with something called "labor."

Brain cells come and brains cells go, but fat cells live forever.

But most of all, remember:

A good friend is like a good bra: hard to find, supportive, comfortable, and always close to your heart!

THINK ABOUT IT

A guy took his blonde girlfriend to her first football game. They had great seats right behind their team's bench. After the game, he asked her how she liked the experience.

"Oh, I really liked it," she replied, "especially the tight pants and all the big muscles, but I just couldn't understand why they were killing each other over twenty-five cents."

Dumbfounded, her date asked, "What do you mean?"

"Well, they flipped a coin, one team got it and then for the rest of the game, all they kept screaming was: "Get the quarterback! Get the quarterback!"

OUTSMARTED

A very wealthy elderly man kept telling his wife that he wanted to take all of his money with him when he died. His wife felt that this was very unfair after forty years of marriage. After resisting this request for several years, she finally promised to honor his request. He died. At the end of an open-casket service, the wife placed a box into the coffin and the coffin was closed and taken away. At that point her close friend, who was aware of the man's request, said, "You didn't really do that, did you?"

The widow answered, "I always keep my promises, so I wrote him a check!"

THE LONGER I LIVE

The longer I live, the more I realize the impact of attitude on life.

It is more important than the past, education, money, circumstances, failures, successes, or what other people think, say, or do. It is more important than appearance, giftedness, or skill. It will make or break a company; a church; a home. The remarkable thing is, we have a choice every day regarding the attitude we will embrace for that day. We cannot change our past... we cannot change the inevitable. The only thing we can do is play on the one string we have, and that is our attitude. I am convinced that life is ten percent what happens to me and ninety percent how I react to it. And so it is with you... we are in charge of our attitudes.

TWINKIES AND ROOT BEER

A little boy wanted to meet God. He knew it was a long trip to where God lived, so he packed his suitcase with Twinkies and a six-pack of root beer and started his journey. When he had gone about three blocks, he met an elderly man. The man was sitting in the park just feeding some pigeons.

The boy sat down next to him and opened his suitcase. He was about to take a drink from his root beer when he noticed that the man looked hungry, so he offered him a Twinkie. The man gratefully accepted it and smiled at the boy. His smile was so pleasant that the boy wanted to see it again, so he offered him a root beer. Again, the man smiled at him. The boy was delighted! They sat there all afternoon eating and smiling, but they never said a word.

As it grew dark, the boy realized how tired he was and got up to leave. Before he had gone more than a few steps, he turned around, ran back to the man, and gave him a hug. The man gave him the biggest smile ever.

When the boy opened the door to his own house a short time later, his mother was surprised by the look of joy on his face. She asked him, "What did you do today that made you so happy?"

He replied, "I had lunch with God." But before his mother could respond, he added, "You know what? God's got the most beautiful smile I've ever seen!"

Meanwhile, the elderly man, also radiant with joy, returned to his home. His son was stunned by the look of peace on his face and he asked, "Dad, what did you do today that made you so happy?"

He replied, "I ate Twinkies in the park with God." However, before his son responded, he added, "You know, he's much younger than I expected."

Too often we underestimate the power of a touch, a smile, a kind word, a listening ear, an honest compliment, or the smallest act of caring, all of which have the potential to turn a life around.

People come into our lives for a reason, a season, or a lifetime. Embrace all equally!

"LITTLE GIRLS"

1. A teacher was giving a lesson on the circulation of the blood. Trying to make the matter clearer, she said, "Now, class, if I stood on my head, the blood, as you know, would run into it, and I would turn red in the face."

   "Yes," the class said.

   "Then why is it that while I am standing upright in the ordinary position, the blood doesn't run into my feet?"

   A little girl shouted, "Cause your feet ain't empty."

2. One day a little girl was sitting and watching her mother do the dishes at the kitchen sink. She suddenly noticed that her mother had several strands of white hair sticking out on her brunette head.

   She looked at her mother and inquisitively asked, "Why are some of your hairs white, Mom?"

   Her mother replied, "Well, every time that you do something wrong and make me cry or unhappy, one of my hairs turns white."

   The little girl thought about this revelation for a while and then said, "Momma, how come *all* grandma's hairs are white?"

3. A kindergarten teacher was observing her classroom of children while they were drawing. She would occasionally walk around to see each child's work.

As she got to one little girl who was working diligently, she asked what the drawing was.

The girl replied, "I'm drawing God."

The teacher paused and said, "But no one knows what God looks like."

Without missing a beat or looking up from her drawing, the girl replied, "They will in a minute."

4. A little girl was talking to her teacher about whales.

The teacher said it was physically impossible for a whale to swallow a human because even though it was a very large mammal, its throat was very small.

The little girl stated that Jonah was swallowed by a whale.

Irritated, the teacher reiterated that a whale could not swallow a human; it was physically impossible.

The little girl said, "When I get to heaven I will ask Jonah."

The teacher asked, "What if Jonah went to hell?"

The little girl replied, "Then, you ask him."

TRIVIA

1. Apples, not caffeine, are most efficient at waking you up in the morning.
2. Alfred Hitchcock didn't have a belly button.
3. A pack-a-day smoker will lose approximately two teeth every ten years.
4. People do not get sick from cold weather; it's from being indoors a lot more.
5. When you sneeze, all bodily functions stop, even your heart!
6. Only seven percent of the population is left-handed.
7. Forty people are sent to the hospital for dog bites every minute.
8. Babies are born without kneecaps. They don't appear until they are two to six years old.
9. The average person over fifty will have spent five years waiting in lines.
10. The toothbrush was invented in 1498.
11. The average housefly lives for one month.
12. Forty thousand Americans are injured by toilets each year.

13. A coat hanger is forty-four inches long when straightened.

14. The average computer user blinks seven times a minute.

15. Your feet are bigger in the afternoon than at any other time of day.

16. Most of us have eaten a spider in our sleep.

17. The real reason ostriches stick their heads in the sand is to search for water.

18. The only two animals that can see behind themselves without turning their heads are the rabbit and the parrot.

19. John Travolta turned down the starring roles in *An Officer and a Gentleman* and *Tootsie.*

20. Michael Jackson owns the rights to the South Carolina state anthem.

21. In most television commercials advertising milk, a mixture of white paint and a little thinner is used in place of the milk.

22. Prince Charles and Prince William *never* travel on the same airplane, just in case there is a crash.

23. The first Harley Davidson motorcycle, built in 1903, used a tomato can for a carburetor.

24. Most hospitals make money by selling the umbilical

cords cut from women who give birth. They are used in vein transplant surgery.

25. Humphrey Bogart was related to Princess Diana. They were seventh cousins.

26. If coloring wasn't added to Coca-Cola, it would be green.

TWO HORSES

Just up the road from my home is a field with two horses in it. From a distance, each looks like every other horse. But if you stop your car or are walking by, you will notice something quite amazing. Looking into the eyes of one horse will disclose that he is blind. His owner has chosen not to have him put down but has made a good home for him.

This alone is amazing.

If nearby and listening, you will hear the sound of a bell. Looking around for the source of the sound, you will see that it comes from the smaller horse in the field. Attached to her halter is a small bell. It lets her blind friend know where she is, so he can follow her.

As you stand and watch these two friends, you'll see how she is always checking on him, and that he will listen for her bell and then slowly walk to where she is, trusting that she will not lead him astray. When she returns to the shelter of the barn each evening, she stops occasionally and looks back, making sure her friend isn't too far behind to hear the bell.

Like the owner of these two horses, God does not throw us away just because we are not perfect or because we have problems or challenges. He watches over us and even brings others into our lives to help us when we are in need. Sometimes we are the blind horse being guided by the little ringing bell of those who God places in our lives.

Other times we are the guide horse, helping others to see. Good friends are like this. You don't always see them, but you know they are always there.

"Be kinder than necessary, for everyone you meet is fighting some kind of battle."

WHY I FIRED MY SECRETARY

Last week was my birthday and I didn't feel very well waking up on that morning. I went downstairs for breakfast hoping my wife would be pleasant and say, "Happy Birthday!" and possibly have a small present for me.

As it turned out, she barely said good morning, let alone, Happy Birthday!

I thought, *Well, that's marriage for you, but the kids... they will remember.*

My kids came bounding downstairs to breakfast and didn't say a word. So when I left for the office, I felt pretty low and somewhat despondent.

As I walked into my office, Jane, my secretary, said, "Good morning, boss, and by the way, Happy Birthday!" I felt a little better that at least someone had remembered. I worked until one o'clock, when Jane knocked on my door and said, "You know, it's such a beautiful day outside, and it is your birthday, what do you say we go out to lunch, just you and me?"

I said, "Thanks, Jane, that's the greatest thing I've heard all day. Let's go!"

We went to lunch. But we didn't go where we normally would go. She chose instead a quiet bistro with a private table. We had two martinis each and I enjoyed the meal tremendously.

On the way back to the office, Jane said, "You know, it's such a beautiful day... we don't need to go straight back to the office, do we?"

I responded, "I guess not. What do you have in mind?"

She said, "Let's drop by my apartment, it's just around the corner."

After arriving at her apartment, Jane turned to me and said, "Boss, if you don't mind, I'm going to step into the bedroom for just a moment. I'll be right back."

"Okay." I nervously replied.

She went into the bedroom and, after a couple of minutes, she came out carrying a huge birthday cake. Followed by my wife, my kids, and a half-dozen of my friends and co-workers, all singing "Happy Birthday."

And, I just stood there ...

Naked!

"QUOTES"

Sometimes, when I look at my children, I say to myself, "Lillian, you should have remained a virgin."

—Lillian Carter (mother of Jimmy Carter)

I had a rose named after me and I was very flattered. But I was not pleased to read the description in the catalog: "No good in a bed, but fine against a wall."

—Eleanor Roosevelt

Last week I stated this woman was the ugliest woman I had ever seen. I have since been visited by her sister, and now wish to withdraw that statement.

—Mark Twain

Santa Claus has the right idea. Visit people only once a year.

—Victor Borge

Be careful about reading health books. You may die of a misprint.

—Mark Twain

By all means, marry. If you get a good wife, you'll become happy; if you get a bad one, you'll become a philosopher.

—Socrates

I was married by a judge. I should have asked for a jury.

—*Groucho Marx*

My wife has a slight impediment in her speech. Every now and then she stops to breathe.

—*Jimmy Durante*

I have never hated a man enough to give his diamonds back.

—*Zsa Zsa Gabor*

Only Irish coffee provides in a single glass all four essential food groups: alcohol, caffeine, sugar, and fat.

—*Alex Levine*

My luck is so bad that if I bought a cemetery, people would stop dying.

—*Rodney Dangerfield*

Money can't buy you happiness, but it does bring you a more pleasant form of misery.

—*Spike Milligan*

Until I was thirteen, I thought my name was *shut up*.

—*Joe Namath*

I don't feel old. I don't feel anything until noon. Then it's time for my nap.

—*Bob Hope*

We can certainly slow the aging process down if it had to work its way through Congress.

—*Will Rogers*

Don't worry about avoiding temptation. As you grow older, it will avoid you.

—*Winston Churchill*

By the time a man is wise enough to watch his step, he's too old to go anywhere.

—*Billy Crystal*

The cardiologist's diet: if it tastes good, spit it out…

—*Anonymous*

GLASS OF MILK

One day, a poor boy who was selling goods from door to door to pay his way through school found he had only one thin dime left, and he was hungry.

He decided he would ask for a meal at the next house. However, he lost his nerve when a lovely young woman opened the door.

Instead of a meal, he asked for a drink of water. She thought he looked hungry so she brought him a large glass of milk. He drank it so slowly, and then asked, "How much do I owe you?"

"You don't owe me anything," she replied. "Mother has taught us never to accept pay for a kindness."

He said, "Then I thank you from my heart."

As Howard Kelly left that house, he not only felt stronger physically, but his faith in God and man was strong also. He had been ready to give up and quit.

Many years later that same young woman became critically ill. The local doctors were baffled. They finally sent her to the big city, where they called in specialists to study her rare disease.

Dr. Howard Kelly was called in for the consultation. When he heard the name of the town she came from, a strange light filled his eyes. Immediately he rose and went down the hall of the hospital to see her room.

Dressed in his doctor's gown he went in to see her. He recognized her at once.

He went back to the consultation room determined to do his best to save her life. From that day he gave special attention to her case.

After a long struggle, the battle was won.

Dr. Kelly requested the business office pass the final bill to him for approval. He looked at it, then wrote something on the edge and the bill was sent to her room. She feared to open it, for she was sure it would take the rest of her life to pay for it all. Finally she looked, and something caught her attention on the side of the bill. She read these words…

"Paid in full with one glass of milk."

(Signed) Dr. Howard Kelly.

Tears of joy flooded her eyes as her happy heart prayed: "Thank you, God, that your love has spread broad through human hearts and hands."

"Bread cast on the waters comes back to you." The good deed you do today may benefit you or someone you love at the least expected time. If you never see the deed again, at least you will have made the world a better place. And, after all, isn't that what life is all about?

WELFARE

A guy walked into the local welfare office to pick up his check. He marched straight up to the counter and said, "Hi. You know, I just *hate* drawing welfare. I'd really rather have a job."

The social worker behind the counter said, "Your timing is excellent. We just got a job opening from a very wealthy old man who wants a chauffeur and bodyguard for his beautiful daughter. You'll have to drive around in his Mercedes, and he'll supply all of your clothes. Because of the long hours, meals will be provided. You'll be expected to escort the daughter on her overseas holiday trips.

You'll be provided a two bedroom apartment above the garage. The salary is $200,000 a year."

The guy, wide-eyed, said, "You're kidding me!"

The social worker said, "Yeah, well... you started it."

TEST FOR DEMENTIA

Below are four questions and a bonus question. You have to answer them instantly. You can't take your time. Answer all of them immediately. Okay?

Let's find out just how clever you really are…

Ready? Go!

First Question:

You are participating in a race. You overtake the second person. What position are you in?

Answer:

If you answered that you are first, then you are absolutely wrong! If you overtake the second person and you take his place, you are second!

Now answer the second question. But don't take as much time as you took for the first question.

Second Question:

If you overtake the last person, then you are…?

Answer:

If you answered that you are second to last, then you are wrong again. Tell me, how can you overtake the *last* person?

Third Question:

Very tricky arithmetic! Note: this must be done in

your head only. Do not use paper and pencil or a calculator. Try it.

Take 1,000 and add 40 to it. Now add another 1,000. Now add 30. Add another 1,000. Now add 20. Now add another 1,000. Now add 10. What is the total?

Answer:

Did you get 5,000? The correct answer is actually 4,100. If you don't believe it, check it with a calculator!

Fourth Question:

Mary's father has five daughters: 1. Nana, 2. Nene, 3. Nini, 4. Nono.

What is the name of the fifth daughter?

Answer:

Did you answer Nunu? No, of course it isn't. Her name is Mary. Read the question again!

Okay, now the bonus round:

A mute person goes into a shop and wants to buy a toothbrush. By imitating the action of brushing his teeth, he successfully expresses himself to the shopkeeper and the purchase is done.

Next, a blind man comes into the shop who wants to buy some aspirin. How does he indicate what he wants?

He just has to open his mouth and ask... It's really very simple. "Pass me the aspirin, please."

IT IS NOT ABOUT YOU …

People are often unreasonable,
Illogical, and self-centered;
Forgive them anyway.

If you are kind,
People may accuse you of selfish, ulterior motives;
Be kind anyway.

If you are successful
You will win some false friends and some true enemies;
Be successful anyway.

If you are honest and frank,
People may cheat you;
Be honest and frank anyway.

What you spend years building,
Someone could destroy overnight;
Build anyway.

If you find serenity and happiness,
They may be jealous;
Be happy anyway.

The good you do today,
People will often forget tomorrow;
Do good anyway.

Give the world the best you have,
And it may never be enough;
Give the world the best you've got anyway.

You see, in the final analysis,
It is between you and God;
It never was about you and them anyway.

YOU ARE IN REAL TROUBLE NOW !

Two little boys, ages eight and ten, are excessively mischievous. They are always getting into trouble and their parents know all about it. If any mischief occurs in their town, the two boys are probably involved.

The boy's mother heard that a new preacher in town had been successful in disciplining children, so she asked if he would speak with her boys. The preacher agreed, but he asked to see them individually. So the mother sent the eight-year-old first, in the morning, with the older boy to see the preacher in the afternoon.

The preacher, a huge man with a deep booming voice, sat the younger boy down and asked him sternly, "Do you know where God is, son?"

The boy's mouth dropped open, but he made no response, sitting there wide-eyed, with his mouth hanging open.

So the preacher repeated the question in an even sterner tone.

"Where is God?"

Again, the boy made no attempt to answer. The preacher raised his voice even more and shook his finger at the boy's face and bellowed.

"Where is God?"

The boy screamed and bolted from the room, ran directly home and dove into his closet, slamming the door behind him.

When his older brother found him in the closet, he asked, "What happened?"

The younger brother, grasping for breath, replied, "We are in *big* trouble this time. *God* is missing and they think we did it!"

Some of us may find a particular environment—whether that is outdoors with nature, or in a church rich in symbols and beauty—conducive to communing with God. Others have a special place they return to for important times of prayer—a particular chair near the window, under a favorite Ponderosa pine on a cliff overlooking the ocean, or whatever. They find that doing so helps them to center in on their relationship with God. It requires self-discipline, adjusted priorities, and relinquishment of old habits to create space for God. It is difficult to make the necessary changes, but great is the benefit of stepping off the treadmill and attending to other things that matter most.

EX WIFE REVENGE !

She spent the first day packing her belongings into boxes, crates, and suitcases. On the second day, she had the movers come and collect her things.

On the third day, she sat down for the last time at their beautiful dining room table by candlelight, put on some soft background music, and feasted on a pound of shrimp, a jar of caviar, and a bottle of chardonnay. When she had finished, she went into each and every room and deposited a few half-eaten shrimp shells, dipped in caviar, into the hollow of the curtain rods. She then cleaned up the kitchen and left.

When the husband returned with his new girlfriend, all was bliss for the first few days. Then, slowly, the house began to smell. They tried everything; cleaning, mopping, and airing the place out. Vents were checked for dead rodents, and carpets were steam cleaned. Air fresheners were hung everywhere. Exterminators were brought in to set off gas canisters, during which they had to move out for a few days, and in the end they even paid to replace the expensive wool carpeting.

Nothing worked. People stopped coming over to visit. Repairmen refused to work in the house. The maid quit. Finally, they could not take the stench any longer and decided to move.

A month later, even though they had cut their price in half, they could not find a buyer for their stinky house.

Word got out, and eventually, even the local realtors refused to return their calls. Finally, they had to borrow a huge sum of money from the bank to purchase a new place.

The ex-wife called the man, and asked how things were going. He told her the saga of the rotting house. She listened politely and said that she missed her old home terribly. She would be willing to reduce her divorce settlement in exchange for getting the house back.

Knowing his ex-wife had no idea how bad the smell was, he agreed on a price that was about one tenth of what the house had been worth, but only if she were to sign the papers that very day. She agreed, and within the hour, his lawyers delivered the paperwork.

A week later, the man and his new girlfriend stood smirking as they watched the moving company pack everything to take to their new home... including the curtain rods.

FAITH IS NOT BELIEVING THAT GOD CAN; IT IS KNOWING THAT GOD WILL!

A few years ago a group of salesmen went to a regional sales convention in Chicago. They had assured their wives that they would be home in plenty of time for Friday night's dinner. In their rush with tickets and briefcases, one of these salesmen inadvertently kicked over a table which held a display of apples. Apples flew everywhere. Without stopping or looking back, they all managed to reach the plane in time for their nearly-missed boarding.

All but one! He paused, took a deep breath, got in touch with his feelings, and experienced a twinge of compassion for the girl whose apple stand had been overturned.

He told his buddies to go on without him, waved goodbye, told one of them to call his wife when they arrived at their home destination and explain his taking a later flight. Then he returned to the terminal where the apples were all over the terminal floor.

He was glad he did.

The sixteen-year-old girl was totally blind! She was softly crying, tears running down her cheeks in frustration, and at the same time helplessly groping for her spilled produce as the crowd swirled about her. No one stopped to care for her plight.

The salesman knelt on the floor with her, gathered up the apples, put them back on the table, and helped her organize her display. As he did this, he noticed that many of them had become battered and bruised; these he set aside in another basket.

When he had finished, he pulled out his wallet and said to the girl, "Here, please take this $40 for the damage we did. Are you okay?" She nodded through her tears. He continued on with, "I hope we didn't spoil your day too badly."

As the salesman started to walk away, the bewildered blind girl called out to him, "Mister…" He paused and turned to look back into those blind eyes. She continued, "Are you Jesus?"

He stopped in mid-stride, and he wondered about her comment. Then slowly he made his way to catch the later flight with that question burning and bouncing about in his soul: "Are you Jesus?"

Do people mistake you for Jesus? That's our destiny, is it not? To be so much like Jesus that people cannot tell the difference as we live and interact with the world that is blind to His love, life, and grace.

If we claim to know Him, we should live, walk and act as He would. Knowing Him is more than simply quoting Scripture and going to church. It's actually living the Word as life unfolds day to day.

You are the apple of His eye. Even though we, too, have been bruised by a fall, He stopped what he was doing and picked you and me up on a hill called Calvary and paid in full for our damaged fruit.

Sometimes we just take things for granted, when we really need to be sharing what we know.

Remember, God never walks away from you…you walk away from Him. And He *always* allows you to come back.

"WHOA TONTO"

An Indian walks into a café with a shotgun in one hand and pulling a male buffalo with the other. He says to the waiter: "Want coffee."

"Sure, Chief. Coming right up."

He gets the Indian a tall mug of coffee. The Indian drinks the coffee down in one gulp, turns, and blasts the buffalo with the shotgun, causing parts of the animal to splatter everywhere. Then he just walks out.

The next morning the Indian returns. He has his shotgun in one hand, pulling another male buffalo with the other. He walks up to the counter and says to the waiter: "Want coffee."

The waiter says, "Whoa, Tonto! We're still cleaning up your mess from yesterday. What was that about, anyway?"

The Indian smiles and proudly says: "Training for position in United States Congress: Come in, drink coffee, shoot the bull, leave mess for others to clean up, disappear for rest of day."

GOOD STUFF

Don't let your worries get the best of you—
remember Moses started out as a basket case …

Some people are kind, polite, and sweet-spirited—
until you try to sit in their pews.

Many folks want to serve God—*but only as advisors.*

It is easier to preach ten sermons—*than it is to live one*

The good Lord didn't create anything with

out a purpose—*but mosquitoes come close!*

When you get to your wit's end—*you'll find God lives there.*
People are funny; they want the front of the bus,
the middle of the road and—*the back of the church!*

Opportunity may knock once—
but temptation bangs on your front door forever!

Quit griping about your church—
if it was perfect, you couldn't belong.

If the church wants a better pastor—
it only needs to pray for the one it has.

God himself does not propose to judge a man
until he is dead—*so, why should you?*

Some minds are like concrete—
thoroughly mixed up and permanently set.

Peace starts with—*a smile.*

I don't know why some people change churches; what
difference does it make which one you stay home from?

A lot of church members who are singing "Stand on the Promises" are just—*sitting on the premises!*

We were called to be witnesses—*not lawyers or judges.*

Be ye fishers of men: you catch them—*he'll clean them.*

Coincidence is when God chooses to remain anonymous.

Don't put a question mark—*where God put a period.*

Don't wait for six strong men to take you to church.

Forbidden fruits create many jams.

God doesn't call the qualified—*he qualifies the called.*

God grades on the cross—*not the curve.*

God loves everyone, but probably prefers "fruits of the spirit" over "religious nuts."

God promises a safe landing, *not a calm passage.*

He who angers you, controls you . . .

If God is your co-pilot—*swap seats!*

Don't give God instructions—*just report for duty!*

The task ahead of us is never as great as—*the power behind us.*

The will of God never takes you to where the grace of God will not protect you.

We don't change the message—*the message changes us.*

You can tell how big a person is by what it takes to discourage him.

The best mathematical equation I have ever seen: *1 cross + 3 nails = 4 given!*

B-I-B-L-E

A father was approached by his small son who told him proudly, "I know what the Bible means!"

His father smiled and replied, "What do you mean, you 'know' what the Bible means?"

The son replied, "I do know!"

"Okay," said his father. "What does the Bible mean?"

"That's easy, Daddy," the young boy replied excitedly. "It stands for 'Basic Information Before Leaving Earth.'"

"10"

There was a very gracious lady who was mailing an old family Bible to her brother in another part of the country.

"Is there anything breakable in here?" asked the postal clerk.

"Only the Ten Commandments," answered the lady.

WHICH ONE ARE YOU?

Somebody has said there are only two kinds of people in the world. There are those who wake up in the morning and say, "Good morning, Lord," and there are those who wake up in the morning and say, "Good Lord, it's morning."

THE CITATION

A minister parked his car in a No Parking zone in a large city because he was short of time and couldn't find a space with a meter. Then he put a note under his windshield wiper that read: "I have circled the block ten times. If I don't park here, I'll miss my appointment. Forgive us our trespasses."

When he returned, he found a citation from a police officer along with this note: "I've circled this block for ten years. If I don't give you a ticket I'll lose my job. Lead us not into temptation."

TITHING

There is a story of a pastor who got up one Sunday and announced to his congregation: "I have good news and bad news. The good news is, we have enough money to pay for our new building program. The bad news is, it's still out there in your pockets."

"LOOK OUT!"

While driving in Pennsylvania, a family caught up to an Amish carriage. The owner of the carriage obviously had a sense of humor, because attached to the back of the carriage was a hand-painted sign: "Energy-efficient vehicle. Runs on oats and grass. Caution: Do not step in exhaust."

"ART"

A Sunday school teacher began her lesson with a question.

"Boys and girls, what do we know about God?"

A hand shot up in the air.

"He's an artist," said the kindergarten boy.

"Really? How do you know?" asked the teacher.

"You know. Our Father, who does art in heaven ..."

WAITING TILL THE LAST MINUTE

A minister waited in line to have his car filled with gas just before a long holiday weekend. The attendant worked quickly, but there were many cars ahead of him. Finally, the attendant motioned him toward a vacant pump.

"Reverend," said the young man. "I'm sorry about the delay. It seems as if everyone waits until the last minute to get ready for a long trip."

The minister chuckled, "I know what you mean. It's the same in my business."

QUILT

Sunday after church, a mom asked her very young daughter what the lesson was about. The daughter answered, "Don't be scared, you'll get your quilt."

Needless to say, the mom was perplexed. Later in the day, the pastor stopped by for tea and the mom asked what that morning's Sunday school lesson was about.

He said, "Be not afraid, thy Comforter is coming."

"PLEASE STAND UP!"

The minister was preoccupied with thoughts of how he was going to ask the congregation to come up with more money than they were expecting for repairs to the church building. Therefore, he was annoyed to find that the regular organist was sick and a substitute had been brought in at the last minute. The substitute wanted to know what to play.

"Here's a copy of the service," he said impatiently. "But you'll have to think of something to play after I make the announcement about the finances."

During the service, the minister paused and said, "Brothers and sisters, we are in great difficulty; the roof repairs cost twice as much as we expected and we need $4,000 more. Any of you who can pledge $100 or more, please stand up."

At that moment, the substitute organist played "The Star-Spangled Banner."

And that is how the substitute became the regular organist.

DANIEL'S STORY

I sat with two friends in the picture window of a quaint restaurant just off the corner of the town square. The food and the company were both especially good that day.

As we talked, my attention was drawn outside, across the street. There, walking into town, was a man who appeared to be carrying all his worldly goods on his back. He was carrying a well-worn sign that read, "I will work for food."

My heart sank.

I brought him to the attention of my friends and noticed that others around us had stopped eating to focus on him. Heads moved in a mixture of sadness and disbelief.

We continued with our meal, but his image lingered in my mind. We finished our meal and went our separate ways. I had errands to do and quickly set out to accomplish them. I glanced toward the town square, looking somewhat half-heartedly for the strange visitor. I was fearful, knowing that seeing him again would call some response. I drove through town and saw nothing of him. I made some purchases at a store and got back into my car.

Deep within me, the Spirit of God kept speaking to me: "Don't go back to the office until you've at least driven once more around the square."

Then, with some hesitancy, I headed back into town. As I turned the square's third corner, I saw him. He was standing on the steps of the storefront church, going through his sack.

I stopped and looked, feeling both compelled to speak to him, yet wanting to drive on. The empty parking space on the corner seemed to be a sign from God; an invitation to park. I pulled in, got out, and approached the town's newest visitor.

"Looking for the pastor?" I asked.

"Not really," he replied, "just resting."

"Have you eaten today?"

"Oh, I ate something early this morning."

"Would you like to have lunch with me?"

"Do you have some work I could do for you?"

"No work," I replied. "I commute here to work from the city, but I would like to take you to lunch."

"Sure," he replied with a smile.

As he began to gather his things, I asked some surface questions.

"Where you headed?"

"St. Louis."

"Where you from?"

"Oh, all over; mostly Florida . . ."

"How long have you been walking?"

"Fourteen years," came the reply.

I knew I had met someone unusual. We sat across from each other in the same restaurant I had left earlier. His face was weathered slightly beyond his thirty-eight years. His eyes were dark, yet clear, and he spoke with an eloquence and articulation that was startling. He removed his jacket to reveal a bright red T-shirt that said, "Jesus is the Never Ending Story."

Then Daniel's story began to unfold. He had seen rough times early in life. He'd made some wrong choices and reaped the consequences. Fourteen years earlier, while backpacking across the country, he had stopped on the beach in Daytona. He tried to hire on with some men who were putting up a large tent and some equipment. A concert, he thought.

He was hired, but the tent would not house a concert but revival services, and in those services he saw life more clearly. He gave his life over to God.

"Nothing has been the same since," he said. "I felt the Lord telling me to keep walking, and so I did, some 14 years now."

"Ever think of stopping?" I asked.

"Oh, once in a while, when it seems to get the best of me. But God has given me this calling. I give out Bibles. That's what's in my sack. I work to buy food and Bibles, and I give them out when His Spirit leads."

I sat amazed. My homeless friend was not homeless. He was on a mission and lived this way by choice. The question burned inside for a moment and then I asked, "What's it like?"

"What?"

"To walk into a town carrying all your things on your back and to show your sign?"

"Oh, it was humiliating at first. People would stare and make comments. Once someone tossed a piece of half-eaten bread and made a gesture that certainly didn't make me feel welcome. But then it became humbling to realize that God was using me to touch lives and change people's concepts of other folks like me."

My concept was changing, too. We finished our dessert and gathered his things. Just outside the door, he paused. He turned to me and said, "Come ye blessed of my Father and inherit the kingdom I've prepared for you. For when I was hungry you gave me food, when I was thirsty you gave me drink, a stranger and you took me in."

I felt as if we were on holy ground.

"Could you use another Bible?" I asked.

He said he preferred a certain translation. It traveled well and was not too heavy. It was also his personal favorite.

"I've read through it fourteen times," he said.

"I'm not sure we've got one of those, but let's stop by our church and see." I was able to find my new friend a Bible that would do well, and he seemed very grateful.

"Where are you headed from here?" I asked.

"Well, I found this little map on the back of this amusement park coupon."

"Are you hoping to hire on there for a while?"

"No, I just figure I should go there. I figure someone under that star right there needs a Bible, so that's where I'm going next."

He smiled, and the warmth of his spirit radiated the sincerity of his mission. I drove him back to the town square where we'd met two hours earlier, and as we drove, it started raining. We parked and unloaded his things.

"Would you sign my autograph book?" he asked. "I like to keep messages from folks I meet."

I wrote in his little book that his commitment to his calling had touched my life. I encouraged him to stay strong. And I left him with a verse of scripture from Jeremiah, "I know the plans I have for you," declared the Lord, "plans to prosper you and not to harm you; plans to give you a future and a hope."

"Thanks, man," he said. "I know we just met and we're really just strangers, but I love you."

"I know," I said. "I love you too. The Lord is good!"

"Yes, he is."

"How long has it been since someone hugged you?" I asked.

"A long time," he replied.

And so on the busy street corner in the drizzling rain, my new friend and I embraced. I felt deep inside that I had been changed. He put his things on his back, smiled his winning smile and said, "See you in the New Jerusalem."

"I'll be there!" was my reply.

He began his journey again. He headed away with his sign dangling from his bedroll and pack of Bibles. He stopped, turned, and said, "When you see something that makes you think of me, will you pray for me?"

"You bet," I shouted back. "God bless."

"God bless."

And that was the last I saw of him.

Late that evening as I left my office, the wind blew strong. The cold front had settled hard upon the town. I bundled up and hurried to my car. As I sat back and reached for the emergency brake, I saw them: a pair of well-worn brown work gloves neatly laid over the length of the handle. I picked them up and thought of my friend and wondered if his hands would stay warm that night without them.

Then I remembered his words: "If you see something that makes you think of me, will you pray for me?"

Today his gloves lie on my desk in my office. They help me to see the world and its people in a new way, and they help me remember those two hours with my unique friend and to pray for his ministry.

"See you in the New Jerusalem," he said. Yes, Daniel, I know I will…

"I shall pass this way but once. Therefore, any good that I can do or any kindness that I can show, let me do it now, for I shall not pass this way again."

Being happy doesn't mean that everything is perfect. It just means that you have decided to see beyond the imperfections.

GRAVEYARD MUSIC

A tourist in Vienna is going through a graveyard when all of a sudden he hears music playing. No one is around, so he starts investigating the source. He finally locates the origin and finds it is coming from a grave with a headstone that reads:

LUDWIG van BEETHOVEN, 1770—1827

It's only then that he realizes that the music playing is his Ninth Symphony and it is being played backward!

Puzzled, he leaves the graveyard and persuades a friend to return with him. By the time they arrive back at the grave the music has changed. This time, it is the Seventh Symphony. But, like the previous piece, it too is being played backward.

Curious, the men agree to consult a music scholar. When they return with the expert, the Fifth Symphony is playing, again backward. The expert makes note that the symphonies are being played in the reverse order in which they were composed, the Ninth, then the Seventh, then the Fifth. By the next day the word has spread, and a throng has gathered around the grave.

They all are listening to the Second Symphony, also being played backward. It's only then that the graveyard's caretaker ambles up to the group. Someone in the crowd asks him if he has an explanation for the music.

"Oh, it's nothing to worry about," says the caretaker. "He's just decomposing!"

TO ALL THE KIDS WHO SURVIVED THE 1930s, '40s, '50s, '60s, & '70s

First, we survived being born to mothers who smoked and drank while they were pregnant.

They took aspirin, ate bleu cheese dressing, tuna from a can, and didn't get tested for diabetes.

Then after that trauma, we were put to sleep on our tummies in baby cribs covered with bright-colored lead-based paints.

We had no childproof lids on medicine bottles, doors, or cabinets.

When we rode our bikes, we had no helmets, not to mention the risks we took hitchhiking.

As infants and children, we would ride in cars with no car seats, booster seats, seat belts, or air bags. Riding in the back of a pickup on a warm day was always a special treat.

We drank water from the garden hose and *not* from a bottle.

We shared one soft drink with four friends from one bottle and *no one* actually died from this.

We ate cupcakes, white bread, and real butter. We drank Kool-aid made with sugar, but we weren't overweight because we were *always outside playing!*

We would leave home in the morning and play all

day, as long as we were back when the streetlights came on.

No one was able to reach us all day.

And we were okay…

We would spend hours building our go-carts out of scraps and then ride down the hill, only to find out we forgot the brakes. After running into the bushes a few times, we learned to solve the problem.

We did not have PlayStations, Nintendos, or Xboxes; no video games at all. No 150 channels on cable, no video movies or DVDs, no surround sound or CDs, no cell phones, no personal computers, no Internet or chat rooms…We had friends and we went outside and found them.

We fell out of trees, got cut, broke bones and teeth, and there were no lawsuits from these accidents.

We ate worms and mud pies made from dirt. The worms did not live in us forever.

We were given BB guns for our tenth birthdays, made up games with sticks and tennis balls, and, although we were told it would happen, we did not put out very many eyes.

We rode bikes or walked to a friend's house. We knocked on the door, rang the bell, or just walked in and talked to them.

Little League had tryouts and not everyone made the team. Those who didn't had to learn to deal with disappointment. Imagine that!

The idea of a parent bailing us out if we broke the law was unheard of. They actually sided with the law.

These generations have produced some of the best risk-takers, problem-solvers, and inventors ever.

The past fifty years have been an explosion of innovation and new ideas.

We had freedom, failure, success, and responsibility, and we learned how to deal with it all.

If you are one of them ... *congratulations!*

Share this with others who have had the luck to grow up as kids before the lawyers and the government regulated so much of our lives. And, while you are at it, show it to your kids so they will know how brave (and lucky) their parents were.

"With hurricanes, tornados, fires out of control, mudslides, flooding, severe thunderstorms tearing up the country from one end to another, and with the threat of bird flu, swine flu and terrorist attacks, are we sure this is a good time to take God out of the Pledge of Allegiance?"

GOOD REASON

A Florida senior citizen drove his brand-new Corvette convertible out of the dealership. Taking off down the road, he pushed it to 80mph, enjoying the wind blowing through what little hair he had left.

Amazing, he thought as he flew down I-75, pushing the pedal even more.

Looking in his rearview mirror, he saw the state trooper behind him, blue lights flashing and siren blaring.

He floored it to 100mph, then 110, then 120. Suddenly he thought, "What am I doing? I'm too old for this!" and he pulled over to await the trooper's arrival.

Pulling in behind him, the trooper walked up to the Corvette, looked at his watch, and said, "Sir, my shift ends in thirty minutes. Today is Friday. If you can give me a reason for speeding that I've never heard before, I'll let you go."

The old man paused and said, "Three years ago, my wife ran off with a Florida State Trooper. I thought you were bringing her back."

"You have a good day, sir," replied the trooper.

IMPACT

One day, when I was a freshman in high school, I saw a kid from my class walking home from school.

His name was Kyle. It looked like he was carrying all of his books.

I thought to myself, "Why would anyone bring home all their books on a Friday? He must really be a nerd."

I had quite a weekend planned—parties and a football game with my friends tomorrow afternoon, so I shrugged my shoulders and went on.

As I was walking, I saw a bunch of kids running toward him. They ran at him, knocking all his books out of his arms, and tripping him so he landed in the dirt.

His glasses went flying and I saw them land in the grass about ten feet from him.

He looked up and I saw this terrible sadness in his eyes. My heart went out to him. So, I jogged over to him as he crawled around looking for his glasses, and I saw a tear in his eye.

As I handed him his glasses, I said, "Those guys are jerks. They really should get lives."

He looked at me and said, "Hey, thanks."

There was a big smile on his face. It was one of those smiles that showed real gratitude.

I helped him pick up his books, and asked him where he lived. As it turned out, he lived near me. So, I asked him why I had never seen him before.

He said he had gone to private school before now.

I would have never hung out with a private school kid before.

We talked all the way home and I carried some of his books. He turned out to be a pretty cool kid.

I asked him if he wanted to play a little football with my friends. He said yes.

We hung out all weekend and the more I got to know Kyle, the more I liked him. And my friends thought the same of him.

Monday morning came and there was Kyle with the huge stack of books again. I stopped him and said, "Boy, you are gonna really build some serious muscles with this pile of books every day."

He just laughed and handed me half the books.

Over the next four years Kyle and I became best friends. When we were seniors we began to think about college.

Kyle decided on Georgetown and I was going to Duke. I knew that we would always be friends, that the miles would never be a problem.

He was going to be a doctor and I was going for business on a football scholarship.

Kyle was valedictorian of our class. I teased him all the time about being a nerd.

He had to prepare a speech for graduation. I was so glad it wasn't me having to get up there and speak.

Graduation day I saw Kyle. He looked great. He was one of those guys that really found himself during high school. He filled out and actually looked good in glasses.

He had more dates than I had and all the girls loved

him. Boy, sometimes I was jealous! Today was one of those days.

I could see that he was nervous about his speech. So, I smacked him on the back and said, "Hey, big guy, you'll be great!"

He looked at me with one of those looks (the really grateful one) and smiled.

"Thanks," he said.

As he started his speech, he cleared his throat and began: "Graduation is a time to thank those who helped you make it through those tough years: your parents, your teachers, your siblings, maybe a coach, but mostly... your friends.

"I am here to tell all of you that being a friend to someone is the best gift you can give them. I am going to tell you a story."

I just looked at my friend with disbelief as he told the story of the first day we met. He had planned to kill himself over the weekend.

He talked of how he had cleaned out his locker so his Mom wouldn't have to do it later and was carrying his stuff home.

He looked hard at me and gave me a little smile.

"Thankfully, I was saved. My friend saved me from doing something unthinkable."

I heard the gasp go through the crowd as this handsome, popular boy told us all about his weakest moment.

I saw his Mom and Dad looking at me and smiling that same grateful smile. Not until that moment did I realize its depth.

Never underestimate the power of your actions. With one small gesture you can change a person's life for better or worse.

God puts us all in each other's lives to impact one another in some way. Look for God in others.

Friends are angels who lift us to our feet when our wings have trouble remembering how to fly.

There is no beginning or end. Yesterday is history, tomorrow is a mystery, and today is a gift.

RAMBLINGS OF A RETIRED MIND

I was thinking that a status symbol of today is those cell phones that everyone has clipped onto their belt or purse. I can't afford one. So, I'm wearing my garage door opener. I also made a cover for my hearing aid, and now I have what they call a bluetooth, I think.

You know, I spent a fortune on deodorant before I realized that people didn't like me anyway.

I was thinking that women should put pictures of missing husbands on beer cans!

I've gotten that dreaded furniture disease. That's when your chest is falling into your drawers!

When people see a cat's litter box, they always say, "Oh, have you got a cat?" Just once I want to say, "No, it's for company!"

Employment application blanks always ask who is to be notified in case of an emergency. I think you should write, "A good doctor."

LISTEN TO THE WHISPER OF GOD

A young man had been to Wednesday night Bible study. The pastor had shared about listening to God and obeying the Lord's voice. The young man couldn't help but wonder, "Does God still speak to people?"

After the service, he went out with some friends for coffee and pie and they discussed the message. Several different ones talked about how God had led them in different ways.

It was about ten o'clock when the young man started driving home. Sitting in his car, he just began to pray, "God, if you still speak to people, speak to me. I will listen. I will do my best to obey."

As he drove down the main street of his town, he had the strangest thought to stop and buy a gallon of milk. He shook his head and said out loud, "God, is that you?" He didn't get a reply and started toward home. But again he thought, *buy a gallon of milk.*

The young man thought about Samuel and how he didn't recognize the voice of God and how little Samuel ran to Eli.

"Okay, God, in case that is you, I will buy the milk."

It didn't seem like too hard a test of obedience. He could always use the milk. He stopped and purchased the gallon of milk and started off toward home.

As he passed Seventh Street, he again felt the urge—*turn down that street.* This is crazy, he thought, and drove on past the intersection.

Again, he felt that he should turn down Seventh Street. At the next intersection, he turned back and headed down Seventh. Half jokingly, he said out loud, "Okay, God, I will."

He drove several blocks, when suddenly, he felt like he should stop. He pulled over to the curb and looked around. He was in a semi-commercial area of town. It wasn't the best, but it wasn't the worst neighborhood either. The businesses were closed and most of the houses looked dark, like the people were already in bed.

Again, he sensed something. *Go and give the milk to the people in the house across the street.* The young man looked at the house. It was dark and it looked like the people were either gone or they were already asleep. He started to open the door and then sat back in the car seat.

"Lord, this is insane. Those people are asleep and if I wake them up, they are going to be mad and I will look stupid." Again, he felt like he should go and give the milk.

Finally, he opened the door.

"Okay, God, if this is you, I will go to the door and I will give them the milk. If you want me to look like a crazy person, okay. I want to be obedient. I guess that will count for something, but if they don't answer right away, I am out of here."

He walked across the street and rang the bell. He could hear some noise inside. A man's voice yelled out, "Who is it? What do you want?" The door opened before the young man could get away.

The man was standing there in his jeans and T-shirt. He looked like he just got out of bed. He had a strange look on his face and he didn't seem too happy to have some stranger on his doorstep.

"What is it?"

The young man thrust out the gallon of milk.

"Here, I brought this for you." The man took the milk and rushed down a hallway.

Then from down the hall came a woman carrying the milk toward the kitchen. The man was following her holding a baby. The baby was crying. The man had tears streaming down his face.

The man began speaking and half-crying, "We were just praying. We had some big bills this month and we ran out of money. We didn't have any milk for our baby. I was just praying and asking God to show me how to get some milk."

His wife in the kitchen yelled out, "I asked him to send an angel with some milk. Are you an angel?"

The young man reached into his wallet and pulled out all the money he had on him and put it in the man's hand. He turned and walked back toward his car. The tears were streaming down his face. He knew that God still answered prayers.

The will of God will never take you where
the grace of God will not protect you.

OKAY!

Three presidential candidates were flying to a debate.

The first one looked at the other two, chuckled, and said, "You know, I could throw a $1,000 bill out of the window right now and make somebody very happy."

The second one shrugged his shoulders and replied, "I could throw ten $100 bills out of the window and make ten people very happy."

The third one added, "That being the case, I could throw one hundred $10 bills out the window and make a hundred people very happy."

Hearing their exchange, the pilot rolled his eyes and said to his copilot, "Such big shots back there. I could throw all three of them out of the window and make 156 million people very happy."

SMOKE SIGNALS

The only survivor of a shipwreck was washed up on a small, uninhabited island. He prayed feverishly for God to rescue him. Every day he scanned the horizon for help, but none seemed forthcoming. Exhausted, he eventually managed to build a little hut out of driftwood to protect himself from the elements and store his few possessions. One day, after scavenging for food, he arrived home to find his little hut in flames with smoke rolling up to the sky. He felt the worst had happened and everything was lost. He was stunned with disbelief, grief, and anger. He cried out, "God! How can you do this to me?"

Early the next day, he was awakened by the sound of a ship approaching the island. It had come to rescue him.

"How did you know I was here?" asked the weary man of his rescuers.

"We saw your smoke signal," they replied.

The Moral of the Story:

It is easy to get discouraged when things are going bad, but we shouldn't lose heart, because God is at work in our lives, even in the midst of our pain and suffering.

Remember that, the next time your little hut seems to be burning to the ground.

It just may be a smoke signal that summons the grace of God.

SKINNY DIPPING

An elderly man in North Carolina had owned a large farm for several years. He had a large pond in the back fixed up really nice with some picnic tables, horseshoe courts, and some apple and peach trees. The pond was properly shaped and fixed up for swimming when it was built.

One evening the old farmer decided to go down to the pond and, as he hadn't been there for a while, look it over. He grabbed a five-gallon bucket to bring back some fruit.

As he neared the pond, he heard voices shouting and laughing with glee. When he came closer, he realized it was a bunch of young women skinny-dipping in his pond. He made the women aware of his presence and they all went to the deep end to shield themselves.

One of the women shouted to him, "We're not coming out until you leave!"

The old man frowned and replied, "I didn't come down here to watch you ladies swim naked or make you get out of the pond naked."

Holding the bucket up, he said, "I'm here to feed the alligator."

DOUGHBOY OBITUARY

Dear Friends,

It is with the saddest heart I pass on the following: please join me in remembering a great icon—the veteran Pillsbury spokesman.

The Pillsbury Doughboy died yesterday of a yeast infection and complications from repeated pokes in the belly. He was 71. Doughboy was buried in a lightly greased coffin. Dozens of celebrities turned out to pay their respects, including Mrs. Butterworth, Hungry Jack, the California Raisins, Betty Crocker, the Hostess Twinkies, and Captain Crunch. The gravesite was piled high with flours.

Longtime friend Aunt Jemima delivered the eulogy, describing Doughboy as a man who never knew how much he was kneaded. Doughboy rose quickly in show business, but his later life was filled with turnovers.

He was not considered a very "smart" cookie, wasting much of his dough on half-baked schemes. Despite being a little flaky at times, he, even as a crusty old man, was considered a roll model for millions. Toward the end it was thought he would rise again, but alas, he was no tart.

Doughboy is survived by his wife, Play Dough; two children, John Dough and Jane Dough; plus they had one in the oven. He is also survived by his elderly father, Pop Tart.The funeral was held at 3:50 for about twenty minutes.

A miracle is not the suspension of natural law,
but the operation of a higher law.

God is the same today as He was yesterday,
and He is still in the miracle business.
If you need a miracle from God, just ask.

Don't know how to find God? Get on
your knees and ask Him to save you.

He will change your life.

May God save you, bless you and give you your miracle.

We ask this in the sweet name of Jesus.
Jesus loves you!

A RIDDLE FOR YOU

When God made Adam out of dust, he thought it best to make me first. So I was made before man, according to God's holy plan. A living being I became and Adam gave to me my name. From his presence I then withdrew, and of me Adam never knew. I did my Maker's law obey, never from it went I astray. Thousand of miles I go in fear, but seldom on earth do I appear. For purpose wise, which God did see, he put a living soul in me. This soul from me that soul I gave, I was as when first made. Without hands or feet or soul, I travel now from pole to pole; I labor hard by day and night, supplying man with great light. Thousands of people, both young and old do by my death great light behold. No right or wrong can I conceive, the scripture I cannot believe. Although my name is therein found, they are to me an empty sound. No fear of death doth trouble me, no happiness I'll ever see. To heaven I will never go, nor down to hell so far below. Now when these lines you slowly read, go search your Bible with all speed. Four times my name is written there I honestly to you declare.

answer: the whale

SPECIAL DELIVERY

I was walking around in a department store when I saw a cashier hand this little boy some money back.

The boy couldn't have been more than five or six years old.

The cashier said, "I'm sorry, but you don't have enough money to buy this doll."

Then the little boy turned to the old woman next to him: "Granny, are you sure I don't have enough money?"

The old lady replied: "You know that you don't have enough money to buy this doll, my dear."

Then she asked him to stay there for a few minutes while she went to look for something.

The little boy was still holding the doll in his hand.

Finally, I walked toward him and I asked him who he wished to give this doll to.

"It's the doll that my sister loved most and wanted so much for Christmas.

She was sure that Santa Claus would bring it to her."

I replied to him that maybe Santa Claus would bring it to her after all, and not to worry.

But he replied to me sadly, "No, Santa Claus can't bring it to her where she is now. I have to give the doll to my mommy so that she can give it to my sister when she goes there."

His eyes were so sad while saying this.

"My sister has gone to be with God. Daddy says that Mommy is going to see God very soon too, so I thought that she could take the doll with her to give to my sister."

My heart nearly stopped.

The little boy looked up at me and said: "I told Daddy to tell Mommy not to go yet. I need her to wait until I come back from the mall."

Then he showed me a very nice photo of himself. He was laughing. He then told me, "I want Mommy to take my picture with her so she won't forget me."

"I love my Mommy and I wish she didn't have to leave me, but Daddy says that she has to go to be with my little sister."

Then he looked again at the doll with sad eyes, very quietly.

I quickly reached for my wallet and said to the boy, "Suppose we check again, just in case you do have enough money for the doll!"

"Okay," he said, "I hope I do have enough."

I added some of my money to his without him seeing and we started to count it. There was enough for the doll and even some spare money.

The little boy said: "Thank you, God, for giving me enough money!"

Then he looked at me and added, "I asked last night before I went to sleep for God to make sure I had enough money to buy this doll, so that Mommy could give it to my sister. He heard me!"

"I also wanted to have enough money to buy a white rose for my Mommy, but I didn't dare ask God for too much. But he gave me enough to buy the doll and a white rose. My mommy loves white roses."

A few minutes later, the old lady returned and I left with my basket.

I finished my shopping in a totally different state of mind from when I started.

I couldn't get the little boy out of my mind.

Then I remembered a local newspaper article two days ago, which mentioned a drunk man in a truck; who hit a car occupied by a young woman and a little girl.

The little girl died right away, and the mother was left in a critical state. The family had to decide whether to pull the plug on the life-sustaining machine, because the young woman would not be able to recover from the coma.

Was this the family of the little boy?

Two days after this encounter with the little boy, I read in the newspaper that the young woman had passed away.

I couldn't stop myself as I bought a bunch of white roses and I went to the funeral home where the body of the young woman was for the people to see and make last wishes before her burial.

She was there, in her coffin, holding a beautiful white rose in her hand with the photo of the little boy and the doll placed over her chest.

I left the place, teary-eyed, feeling that my life had been changed forever. The love that the little boy had for his mother and his sister is still, to this day, hard to imagine.

A COWBOY NAMED JAKE

A cowboy named Jake was overseeing his herd in a remote pasture in Oklahoma when suddenly a brand new BMW advanced out of a dust cloud towards him.

The driver, a young man in Brioni suit, Gucci shoes, RayBan sun glasses and YSL tie, leans out the window and asks the cowboy, “If I tell you exactly how many cows and calves you have in your herd, will you give me a calf?”

Jake looks at the man, obviously a yuppie, then looks at this peacefully grazing herd and calmly answers, “Sure, why not?”

The yuppie parks his car, whips out his Dell notebook computer, connects it to his Cingular RAZR V3 cell phone, and surfs to a NASA page on the Internet, where he calls up a GPS satellite to get an ultra-high-resolution photo.

The young man then opens the digital photo in Adobe Photoshop and exports it to an image processing facility in Hamburg, Germany.

Within seconds, he receives an email on his Palm Pilot that the image has been processed and the data stored. He then accesses an MS-SQL database through an ODBC-connected Excel spreadsheet with email on his Blackberry and, after a few minutes, receives a response.

Finally, he prints out a full-color, 150-page report on his hi-tech, miniaturized HP LaserJet printer. He finally turns to the cowboy and says, “You have exactly 1,586 cows and calves.”

“That’s right. Well, I guess you can take one of my calves,” says Jake.

He watches the young man select one of the animals and looks on, amused, as the young man stuffs it into the trunk of his car.

Then Jake says to the young man, “Hey, if I can tell you exactly what your business is, will you give me back my calf?”

The young man thinks about it for a second and then says, “Okay, why not?”

“You’re a congressman for the U.S. government,” says Jake.

“Wow! That’s correct,” says the yuppie, “but how did you guess that?”

“No guessing required,” answered the cowboy. ‘You showed up here even though nobody called you; you want to get paid for an answer I already knew, to a question I never asked. You tried to show me how much smarter than me you are; and you don’t know a thing about cows . . . this is a herd of sheep. Now, give me back my dog!”

THE LINCOLN-KENNEDY MYSTERY

Have a history teacher explain this… if they can.

- Abraham Lincoln was elected to Congress in 1846.
- John F. Kennedy was elected to Congress in 1946.
- Abraham Lincoln was elected President in 1860.
- John F. Kennedy was elected President in 1960.
- Both were particularly concerned with civil rights.
- Both wives lost their children while living in the White House.
- Both Presidents were shot on a Friday.
- Both Presidents were shot in the head.

Now, it gets really weird.

- Lincoln's secretary was named Kennedy.
- Kennedy's secretary was named Lincoln.
- Both were assassinated by southerners.
- Both were succeeded by southerners named Johnson.
- Andrew Johnson, who succeeded Lincoln, was born in 1808.
- Lyndon Johnson, who succeeded Kennedy, was born in 1908.
- John Wilkes Booth, who assassinated Lincoln, was born in 1839.
- Lee Harvey Oswald, who assassinated Kennedy, was born in 1939.
- Both assassins were known by their three names.
- Both names are composed of fifteen letters.

Now, hang on to your seat.

- Lincoln was shot at the theater named Ford.
- Kennedy was shot in a car called Lincoln, made by Ford.
- Lincoln was shot in a theater and his assassin hid in a warehouse.
- Kennedy was shot from a warehouse and his assassin hid in a theater.
- Booth and Oswald were both assassinated before their trials.

And here is the kicker…

- A week before Lincoln was shot, he was in Monroe, Maryland.
- A week before Kennedy was shot, he was with Marilyn Monroe.

THE DEVIL AND THE DUCK

There was a little boy visiting his grandparents on their farm.

He was given a slingshot to play with out in the woods.

He practiced in the woods; but he could never hit the target.

Getting a little discouraged, he headed back for dinner.

As he was walking back he saw Grandma's pet duck.

Just out of impulse, he let the slingshot fly, hit the duck square in the head and killed it.

He was so shocked and grieved!

In a panic, he hid the dead duck in the woodpile, only to see his sister watching!

Sally had seen it all, but she said nothing.

After lunch the next day Grandma said, "Sally, let's wash the dishes."

But Sally said, "Grandma, Johnny told me he wanted to help in the kitchen."

Then she whispered to him, "Remember the duck?"

So Johnny did the dishes.

Later that day, Grandpa asked if the children wanted to go fishing and Grandma said, "I'm sorry, but I need Sally to help make supper."

Sally just smiled and said, "Well that's all right, because Johnny told me he wanted to help."

She whispered again, "Remember the duck?"

So, Sally went fishing and Johnny stayed to help.

After several days of Johnny doing both his chores and Sally's, he finally couldn't stand it any longer.

He came to Grandma and confessed that he had killed the duck.

Grandma knelt down, gave him a hug and said, "Sweetheart, I know. You see, I was standing at the window and I saw the whole thing, but because I love you, I forgave you.

I was just wondering how long you would let Sally make a slave of you."

THOUGHT for the day and every day thereafter:

Whatever is in your past, whatever you have done, and the devil keeps throwing it up in your face (lying, cheating, debt, fear, bad habits, hatred, anger, bitterness, etc.); whatever it is, you need to know that:

God was standing at the window and he saw the whole thing.

He has seen your whole life. He wants you to know that he loves you and that you are forgiven. He is just wondering how long you will let the devil make a slave of you.

The great thing about God is that when you ask for forgiveness;

He not only forgives you, but he forgets.

It is by God's grace and mercy that we are saved.

Go ahead and make the difference in someone's life today.

Share this with a friend and always remember:

God is at the window!

When Jesus died on the cross; he was thinking of you & me!

THE BRICK

A young and successful executive was traveling down a neighborhood street, driving a bit too fast in his new Jaguar. He was watching for kids darting out from between parked cars and slowed down when he thought he saw something. As his car passed, no children appeared. Instead, a brick smashed into the Jag's side door! He slammed on the brakes and backed the Jag back to the spot where the brick had been thrown. The angry driver then jumped out of the car, grabbed the nearest kid and pushed him up against a parked car, shouting, "What was all that about and who are you? Just what the heck are you doing? That's a new car and that brick you threw is going to cost a lot of money. Why did you do it?"

The young boy was apologetic.

"Please mister . . . please, I'm sorry, but I didn't know what else to do," he pleaded. "I threw the brick because no one else would stop . . ."

With tears dripping down his face and off his chin, the youth pointed to a spot just around a parked car.

"It's my brother," he said. "He rolled off the curb and fell out of his wheelchair and I can't lift him up."

Now sobbing, the boy asked the stunned executive, "Would you please help me get him back into his wheelchair? He's hurt and he's too heavy for me."

Moved beyond words, the driver tried to swallow the rapidly swelling lump in his throat. He hurriedly lifted the handicapped boy back into the wheelchair, then took out a linen handkerchief and dabbed at the fresh scrapes and cuts. A quick look told him everything was going to be okay.

"Thank you and may God bless you," the grateful child told the stranger. Too shook up for words, the man simply watched the boy push his wheelchair-bound brother down the sidewalk toward their home.

It was a long, slow walk back to the Jaguar. The damage was very noticeable, but the driver never bothered to repair the dented side door. He kept the dent there to remind him of this message: "Don't go through life so fast that someone has to throw a brick at you to get your attention!"

God whispers in our souls and speaks to our hearts.

Sometimes when we don't have time to listen, he has to throw a brick at us.

It's our choice to listen or not.

E-MAIL

A Minneapolis couple decided to go to Florida to thaw out during a particularly icy winter.

They planned to stay at the same hotel where they spent their honeymoon twenty years earlier. Because of their hectic schedules, it was difficult to coordinate their travel schedules. So, the husband left Minnesota and flew to Florida on Thursday, with his wife flying down the following day.

The husband checked into the hotel. There was a computer in his room, so he decided to send an email to his wife.

However, he accidentally left out one letter in her email address, and without realizing his error, sent the email.

Meanwhile, somewhere in Houston, a widow had just returned home from her husband's funeral.

He was a minister who was called home to glory following a heart attack.

The widow decided to check her e-mail, expecting messages from relatives and friends.

After reading the first message, she screamed and fainted.

The widow's son rushed into the room, found his Mother on the floor, and saw the computer screen, which read:

To: My Loving Wife
Subject: I have arrived
Date: October 16, 2007

I know you are surprised to hear from me. They have computers here now and you are allowed to send emails to your loved ones. I have just arrived and have been checked in.

I see that everything has been prepared for your arrival tomorrow.

Looking forward to seeing you then!

Hope your journey is as uneventful as mine was.

P.S ... Sure is hot down here!

THE MOUSE AND THE MOUSTRAP

A mouse looked through the crack in the wall to see the farmer and his wife open a package.

"What food might this contain?" the mouse wondered. He was devastated to discover it was a mousetrap.

Retreating to the farmyard, the mouse proclaimed the warning:

"There is a mousetrap in the house! There is a mousetrap in the house!"

The chicken chuckled, scratched, raised her head and said, "Mr. Mouse, I can tell this is a grave concern to you, but it is of no consequence to me. I cannot be bothered by it."

The mouse turned to the pig and told him, "There is a mousetrap in the house! There is a mousetrap in the house!"

The pig sympathized, but said, "I am sorry, Mr. Mouse, but there is nothing I can do about it but pray. Be assured you are in my prayers."

The mouse turned to the cow and said, "There is a mousetrap in the house! There is a mousetrap in the house!"

The cow said, "Wow, Mr. Mouse. I am sorry for you, but it is no skin off my nose."

So, the mouse returned to the house, head down and dejected, to face the farmer's mousetrap ... alone.

That very night a sound was heard throughout the house, like the sound of a mousetrap catching its prey.

The farmer's wife rushed to see what was caught.

In the darkness, she did not see it was a venomous snake, and its tail was caught by the trap.

The snake bit the farmer's wife.

The farmer rushed her to the hospital, and she returned home with a fever.

Everyone knows you treat a fever with fresh chicken soup, so the farmer took his hatchet to the farmyard for the soup's main ingredient.

But his wife's sickness continued, so friends and neighbors came to sit with her around the clock.

To feed them, the farmer butchered the pig.

The farmer's wife did not get well; she died.

So many people came for her funeral that the farmer had the cow slaughtered to provide enough meat for all of them.

The mouse looked upon it all from his crack in the wall with great sadness.

So, the next time you hear someone is facing a problem and think it doesn't concern you, remember ... When one of us it threatened, we are all at risk. We must keep an eye out for one another and make an extra effort to encourage one another.

LAST IN LINE BUT FIRST TO LAUGH

A bus carrying only ugly people crashes into an oncoming truck, and everyone inside dies.

As they stand at the pearly gates waiting to enter paradise and meet their maker, God decides to grant each person one wish because of the grief they have experienced.

They are all lined up, and God asks the first one what the wish is.

"I want to be gorgeous."

So God snaps His fingers and it is done.

The second one in line hears this and says, "I want to be gorgeous too."

Another snap of his fingers and the wish is granted.

This goes on for a while, with each one asking to be gorgeous. But when God is halfway down the line, the last guy in the line starts laughing.

When there are only ten people left, this guy is rolling on the floor, laughing his head off.

Finally, God reaches this last guy and asks him what his wish will be.

The guy eventually calms down and says:

"Make them all ugly again!"

Next time you are last in line. Be happy!

FEEDING SOLDIERS

I put my carry-on in the luggage compartment and sat down in my assigned seat. It was going to be a long flight. *I'm glad I have a good book to read. Perhaps I will get a short nap,* I thought.

Just before take-off, a line of soldiers came down the aisle and filled all the vacant seats, totally surrounding me. I decided to start a conversation.

"Where are you headed?" I asked the soldier seated nearest to me.

"Great Lakes Air Base. We will be there for two weeks for special training, and then we are being deployed to Iraq."

After flying for about an hour, an announcement was made that sack lunches were available for five dollars. It would be several hours before we reached Chicago, and I quickly decided a lunch would help pass the time.

As I reached for my wallet, I overheard a soldier ask his buddy if he planned to buy lunch.

"No, that seems like a lot of money for a sack lunch. Probably wouldn't be worth five bucks. I'll wait till we get to Chicago." His friend agreed.

I looked around at the other soldiers. None were buying lunch. I walked to the back of the plane and handed the flight attendant a fifty-dollar bill.

"Take a lunch to all those soldiers."

She grabbed my arms and squeezed tightly. Her eyes were wet with tears. She thanked me.

"My son was a soldier in Iraq; it's almost like you are doing it for him."

Picking up ten sacks, she headed up the aisle to where the soldiers were seated. She stopped at my seat and asked, "Which do you like best—beef or chicken?"

"Chicken," I replied, wondering why she asked. She turned and went to the front of the plane, returning a minute later with a dinner plate from first class. "This is your thanks."

After we finished eating, I went to the back of the plane, heading for the restroom. A man stopped me. "I saw what you did. I want to be part of it. Here, take this." He handed me twenty-five dollars.

Soon after I returned to my seat, I saw the flight captain coming down the aisle, looking at the aisle numbers as he walked. I hoped he was not looking for me, but noticed he was looking at the numbers only on my side of the plane. When he got to my row he stopped, smiled, held out his hand, and said, "I want to shake your hand."

Quickly unfastening my seat belt I stood and took the Captain's hand. With a booming voice he said, "I was a soldier and I was a military pilot. Once, someone bought me a lunch. It was an act of kindness I never forgot." I was embarrassed when applause was heard from all the passengers.

Later I walked to the front of the plane so I could stretch my legs. A man who was seated about six rows in front of me reached out his hand, wanting to shake mine. He left another twenty-five dollars in my palm.

When we landed in Chicago I gathered my belongings and started to deplane. Waiting just inside the airplane door was a man who stopped me, put something in my shirt pocket, turned, and walked away without saying a word. Another twenty-five dollars!

Upon entering the terminal, I saw the soldiers gathering for their trip to the base. I walked over to them and handed them seventy-five dollars. "It will take you some time to reach the base. It will be about time for a sandwich. God Bless You!"

Ten young men left that flight feeling the love and respect of their fellow travelers. As I walked briskly to my car, I whispered a prayer for their safe return. These soldiers were giving their all for our country. I could only give a couple of meals. It seemed so little...

'TWAS THE NIGHT BEFORE CHRISTMAS

He lived all alone,
In a one bedroom house made of
Plaster and stone.
I had come down the chimney
With presents to give,
And to see just who
In this home did live.
I looked all about,
A strange sight I did see,
No tinsel, no presents,
Not even a tree.
No stocking by the mantle,
Just boots filled with sand,
On the wall hung pictures
Of far-distant lands.
With medals and badges,
Awards of all kinds,
A sober thought
Came through my mind.
For this house was different,
It was dark and dreary,
I found the home of a soldier,
Once I could see clearly.
The soldier lay sleeping,
Silent, alone

Curled up on the floor
In this one bedroom home.
The face was so gentle,
The room in such disorder,
Not how I pictured
A United States Soldier.
Was this the hero
Of whom I had just read?
Curled up on a poncho,
The floor for a bed?
I realized the families
That I saw this night,
Owed their lives to these soldiers
Who were willing to fight.
Soon round the world,
The children would play,
And grownups would celebrate
A bright Christmas Day.
They all enjoyed freedom
Each month of the year,
Because of the soldiers,
Like the one lying here.
I couldn't help wonder
How many lay alone,
On a cold Christmas Eve
In a land far from home.
The very thought
Brought a tear to my eye,
I dropped to my knees
And started to cry.
The soldier awakened

And I heard a rough voice,
"Santa don't cry,
This life is my choice;
I fight for freedom,
I don't ask for more,
My life is God,
My country, my corps."
The soldier rolled over
And drifted to sleep,
I couldn't control it,
I continued to weep.
I kept watch for hours,
So silent and still
And we both shivered
From the cold night's chill.
I didn't want to leave
On that cold, dark, night,
This guardian of honor
So willing to fight.
Then the soldier rolled over,
With a voice soft and pure,
He whispered, "Carry on Santa,
It is Christmas Day, all is secure!"
One look at my watch,
And I knew he was right.
"Merry Christmas my friend,
And to all a good night!"

MY WIFE . . .

My wife sat down on the couch next to me as I was flipping the channels.

"What's on TV?" she asked.

I said, "Dust."

My wife was hinting about what she wanted for our upcoming anniversary.

She said, "I want something shiny that goes from 0 to 200 in about three seconds."

I bought her a scale.

When I got home last night, my wife demanded that I take her somewhere expensive . . .

So, I took her to a gas station.

My wife and I were sitting at a table at my high school reunion, and I kept staring at a drunken lady swigging her drink as she sat alone at a nearby table.

My wife asked, "Do you know her?"

"Yes." I sighed. "She's my old girlfriend. I understand she took to drinking right after we split up those many years ago, and I hear she hasn't been sober since."

"My goodness," says my wife, "who would think a person could go on celebrating that long?"

LITTLE THINGS SEEM FUNNY

I rear-ended a car this morning. So, there we were alongside the road. Slowly, the other driver got out of his car.

You know how sometimes you just get so stressed and little things just seem funny?

Yea, well I couldn't believe it… he was a dwarf!

He stormed over to my car, looked up at me, and shouted, "I am not happy!"

So, I looked down at him and said, "Well, then which one are you?"

THE OTHER IS THE HUSBAND

When our lawn mower broke and wouldn't run, my wife kept hinting to me that I should get it fixed.

But, somehow I always had something else to take care of first: the truck, the car, playing golf, always something more important to me.

Finally, she thought of a clever way to make her point.

When I arrived home one day, I found her seated in the tall grass, busily snipping away with a tiny pair of sewing scissors.

I watched silently for a short time and then went into the house.

I was gone only a minute, and when I came out again I handed her a toothbrush.

I said, "When you finish cutting the grass, you might as well sweep the driveway."

The doctors say I will walk again, but I will always have a limp.

Moral to this story:

Marriage is a relationship in which one person is always right, and the other is the husband.

BORN BEFORE ...

One evening a grandson was talking to his grandfather about current events.

The grandson asked his grandfather what he thought about the shootings at schools, the computer age, and just things in general.

The grandfather replied, "Well, let me think a minute, I was born before:

- Television
- Polio shots
- Frozen foods
- Xerox
- Contact lenses
- Frisbee and
- The pill
- There were no:
- Credit Cards
- Laser beams or
- Ball-point pens
- Man had not invented:
- Pantyhose
- Air conditioners
- Dishwashers

- Clothes Dryers
- And the clothes were hung out to dry in the fresh air and
- Man had not yet walked on the moon.
- Your grandmother and I got married first…
- *And then* lived together.
- Every family had a father and a mother.
- Until I was twenty-five, I called every man older than me, "sir."
- And after I turned twenty-five, I still called policemen and every man with a title, "sir."
- We were born before gay rights, computer dating, dual careers, daycare centers, and group therapy.
- Our lives were governed by the Ten Commandments, good judgment, and common sense.
- We were taught to know the difference between right and wrong, and to stand up and take responsibility of our actions.
- Serving your country was a privilege; living in this country was a bigger privilege.
- We thought fast food was what people ate during Lent.
- Having a meaningful relationship meant getting along with your cousins.
- Draft dodgers were people who closed their front doors when the evening breeze started.
- Time-sharing meant time the family spent together

in the evenings and weekends, not purchasing condominiums.

- We never heard of FM radios, tape decks, CDs, electric typewriters, yogurt, or guys wearing earrings.
- We listened to the big bands, Jack Benny, and the President's speeches on our radios.
- And I don't remember any kid blowing his brains out listening to Tommy Dorsey.
- If you saw anything with "Made in Japan" on it, it was junk.
- The term "making out" referred to how you did on your school exam.
- Pizza Hut, McDonald's, and instant coffee were unheard of.
- We had five & ten cent stores where you could actually buy things for five & ten cents.
- Ice cream cones, phone calls, rides on a street car, and a Pepsi were all a nickel.
- And if you didn't want to splurge, you could spend your nickel on enough stamps to mail one letter and two postcards.
- You could buy a new Chevy Coupe for $600.00 … but who could afford one?
- Too bad, because gas was eleven cents a gallon.
- In my day:
- "Grass" was mowed,
- "Coke" was a cold drink,

- "Pot" was something your mother cooked in and
- "Rock music" was your grandmother's lullaby.
- "Aids" were helpers in the principal's office,
- "Chip" meant a piece of wood,
- "Hardware" was found in a hardware store and
- "Software" wasn't even a word.
- And we were the last generation to actually believe that a lady needed a husband to have a baby.

No wonder people call us "old and confused" and say there is a generation gap . . . And how old do you think I am?

I bet you have an age in mind . . . you are in for a shock!

Pretty scary if you think about it and pretty sad at the same time.

Are you ready?

This man would be only fifty-nine years old!

THE WEIGHT OF PRAYER

A poorly-dressed lady with a look of defeat on her face walked into a grocery store. She approached the owner of the store in a most humble manner and asked if he would let her charge a few groceries.

She softly explained that her husband was very ill and unable to work, yet they had seven children and they needed food.

The grocer scoffed at her and requested that she leave his store at once.

Visualizing the family needs, she said, "Please, sir! I will bring you the money just as soon as I can."

The grocer told her he could not give her credit, since she did not have a charge account at this store.

Standing beside the counter was a customer who overheard the conversation between the two.

The customer walked forward and told the grocer that he would stand good for whatever she needed for her family.

The grocer said in very reluctant voice, "Do you have a grocery list?"

The lady replied, "Yes sir."

"Okay," he said. "Put your grocery list on the scales and whatever your grocery list weighs, I will give you that amount in groceries."

She hesitated a moment with a bowed head, then she reached into her purse and took out a piece of paper and scribbled something on it. She then laid the piece of paper on the scale carefully, with her head still bowed.

The eyes of the grocer and the customer showed amazement when the scales went down and stayed down.

The grocer, staring at the scales, turned slowly to the customer and said begrudgingly, "I can't believe it."

The customer smiled and the grocer started putting the groceries on the other side of the scales. The scale did not balance, so he continued to put more and more groceries on them until the scales would hold no more.

The grocer stood there in utter disgust. Finally, he grabbed the piece of paper from the scales and looked at it with greater amazement.

It was not a grocery list. It was a prayer which said:

"Dear Lord, you know my needs and I am leaving this in your hands."

The grocer gave her the groceries that he had gathered and stood in stunned silence.

The lady thanked him and left the store.

The other customer handed a fifty-dollar bill to the grocer and said, "It was worth every penny of it. Only God knows how much a prayer weighs."

THE POWER OF PRAYER

When you read this, say a prayer. That's all you have to do. Just a prayer of thanks for your own good fortune.

OUTSOURCED HOTLINE

I was very, very depressed last night, so I called the Suicide Prevention Lifeline.

I reached a call center in Pakistan.

I told them I was suicidal.

They got all excited and asked if I could drive a truck or van.

ALL FOR A QUARTER

Several years ago, a preacher from out of state accepted a call to a church in Houston, Texas. Some weeks after he arrived, he had an occasion to ride the bus from his home to the downtown area. When he sat down, he discovered that the driver had accidentally given him a quarter too much in change.

As he considered what to do, he thought to himself, *You better give the quarter back. It would be wrong to keep it.* Then he thought, *Oh, forget it, it's only a quarter. Who would worry about this little amount? Anyway, the bus company gets too much fare; they will never miss it. Accept it as a 'gift from God' and keep quiet.*

When his stop came, he paused momentarily at the door, and then he handed the quarter to the driver and said, "Here, you gave me too much change."

The driver, with a smile, replied, "Aren't you the new preacher in town?"

"Yes," he replied.

"Well, I have been thinking a lot lately about going somewhere to worship. I just wanted to see what you would do if I gave you too much change. I'll see you at church on Sunday."

When the preacher stepped off the bus, he literally grabbed the nearest light pole, held on, and said, "Oh God, I almost sold your Son for a quarter!"

IRREFUTABLE LOGIC

A minister decided that a visual demonstration would add emphasis to his Sunday sermon.

Four worms were placed into four separate jars.

The first worm was put into a container of alcohol.

The second worm was put into a container of cigarette smoke.

The third worm was put into a container of chocolate syrup.

The fourth worm was put into a container of good clean soil.

At the conclusion of the sermon, the minister reported the following results:

The first worm in alcohol: dead.

The second worm in cigarette smoke: dead.

The third worm in chocolate syrup: dead.

The fourth worm in good clean soil: alive.

So the minister asked the congregation:

"What did you learn from this demonstration?"

An elderly woman who was sitting in the back quickly raised her hand and said,

"As long as you drink, smoke, and eat chocolate, you won't have worms!"

WHERE HE BELONGS

A father wanted to read a magazine but was being bothered by his little girl, Shelby.

She wanted to know what the United States looked like.

Finally, he tore a sheet out of his new magazine on which was printed the map of the country.

Tearing it into small pieces, he gave it to Shelby, and said, "Go into the other room and see if you can put this together. This will show you our whole country today."

After a few minutes, Shelby returned and handed him the map, correctly fitted and taped together.

The father was surprised and asked how she had finished so quickly.

"Oh," she said, "on the other side of the paper is a picture of Jesus ... When I got all of Jesus back where he belonged, then our country came together."

Amen!

IF MY BODY WERE A CAR

If my body were a car, I would be thinking about trading it in for a newer model. I have bumps and dents and scratches in my finish, and my paint job is getting a little dull…

But that's not the worst of it.

My headlights are out of focus, and it's hard to see things up close.

My traction is not as graceful as it once was. I slip and slide and skid and bump into things, even in the best of weather. My whitewalls are stained with varicose veins. It takes me longer to reach my maximum speed. My fuel burns inefficiently.

But here's the worst of it…

Almost every time I sneeze, cough or laugh…

Either my radiator leaks or my exhaust backfires!

RANDOM ACTS OF KINDNESS

As she stood in front of her fifth grade class on the very first day of school, she told the children an untruth. Like most teachers, she looked at her students and said she loved them all the same. However, that was impossible, because there in the front row, slumped in his seat, was a little boy named Teddy Stoddard.

Mrs. Thompson had watched Teddy the year before and noticed that he did not play well with the other children, that his clothes were messy, and that he constantly needed a bath. In addition, Teddy could be unpleasant. It got to the point where Mrs. Thompson would actually take delight in marking bold X's and putting a big "F" at the top of his paper.

At the school where Mrs. Thompson taught, she was required to review each child's past records, and she put Teddy's off until last. However, when she reviewed his file, she was in for a surprise

Teddy's first grade teacher wrote, "Teddy is a bright child with a ready laugh. He does his work neatly and has good manners ... he is a joy to be around."

His second grade teacher wrote, "Teddy is an excellent student, well-liked by his classmates, but he is troubled because his mother has a terminal illness and life at home must be a struggle."

His third grade teacher wrote, "His mother's death has been hard on him. He tries to do his best, but his father doesn't show much interest, and his home life will soon affect him if some steps are not taken."

Teddy's fourth grade teacher wrote, "Teddy is withdrawn and does not show much interest in school. He does not have many friends and he sometimes sleeps in class."

By now, Mrs. Thompson realized the problem and she was ashamed of herself. She felt even worse when her students brought her Christmas presents, wrapped in beautiful ribbons and bright paper, except for Teddy's. His present was clumsily wrapped in the heavy, brown paper that he got from a grocery bag. Mrs. Thompson took pains to open it in the middle of the other presents. Some of the children started to laugh when she found a rhinestone bracelet with some of the stones missing, and a bottle that was one-quarter full of perfume. But she stifled the children's laughter when she exclaimed how pretty the bracelet was, putting it on, and dabbing some of the perfume on her wrist. Teddy Stoddard stayed after school that day just long enough to say, "Mrs. Thompson, today you smelled just like my Mom used to."

After the children left, she cried for at least an hour. On that very day, she quit teaching reading, writing, and arithmetic. Instead, she began to teach children.

Mrs. Thompson paid particular attention to Teddy. As she worked with him, his mind seemed to come alive. The more she encouraged him, the faster he responded. By the end of the year, Teddy had become one of the smartest children in the class and, despite her lie that she would love all the children the same, Teddy became one of her "teacher's pets."

A year later, she found a note under her door, from

Teddy, telling her that she was the best teacher he ever had in his whole life.

Six years went by before she got another note from Teddy. He then wrote that he had finished high school, third in his class, and she was still the best teacher he ever had in his life.

Four years after that, she got another letter, saying that while things had been tough at times, he'd stayed in school, had stuck with it, and would soon graduate from college with the highest of honors. He assured Mrs. Thompson that she was still the best and favorite teacher he had ever had in his whole life.

Then four more years passed and yet another letter came. This time he explained that after he got his bachelor's degree, he decided to go a little further. The letter explained that she was still the best and favorite teacher he ever had. But now his name was a little longer ... The letter was signed, Theodore F. Stoddard, MD.

The story does not end there. You see, there was yet another letter that spring. Teddy said he had met this girl and was going to be married. He explained that his father had died a couple of years ago and he was wondering if Mrs. Thompson might agree to sit at the wedding in the place that was usually reserved for the mother of the groom. Of course, Mrs. Thompson did. And guess what? She wore that bracelet, the one with several rhinestones missing. Moreover, she made sure she was wearing the perfume that Teddy remembered his mother wearing on their last Christmas together.

They hugged each other, and Dr. Stoddard whispered in Mrs. Thompson's ear, "Thank you Mrs. Thompson, for believing in me. Thank you so much for making me feel important and showing me that I could make a difference."

Mrs. Thompson, with tears in her eyes, whispered back. She said, "Teddy, you have it all wrong. You were the one who taught me that I could make a difference. I didn't know how to teach until I met you."

(For those of you that don't know, Teddy Stoddard is the doctor at Iowa Methodist in Des Moines that has the Stoddard Cancer Wing.)

Warm someone's heart today... pass this story along. I love this story so very much, I cry every time I read it. Let's try to make a difference in someone's life today.

Random acts of kindness, I think they call it.

ITALIAN TOMATO GARDEN

There was an old Italian man who lived alone. He wanted to plant his annual tomato garden, but it was very difficult work, as the ground was hard. His only son, Vincent, who used to help him, was in prison. The old man wrote a letter to his son and described his predicament:

> Dear Vincent,
>
> I am feeling pretty sad, because it looks like I won't be able to plant my tomato garden this year. I'm just getting too old to be diggig up a garden plot. I know if you were here my trouble would be over…I know you would be happy to dig the plot for me, like in the good old days.
>
> Love, Papa

A few days later he received a letter from his son.

> Dear Pop,
>
> Don't dig up that garden. That's there the bodies are buried.
>
> Love,
> Vinnie

At 4am the next morning, FBI agents and local police arrived and dug up the entire area without finding any bodies. They apologized to the old man and left.

That same day the old man received another letter from his son.

Dear Pop,

Go ahead and plant tomatoes now. That's the best I could do under the circumstances.

Love you,
Vinnie

LIFE IS LIKE A ROLL OF TOILET PAPER

Life is like a roll of toilet paper.

The closer it gets to the end, the faster it goes.

So …

Have fun, think good thoughts only, learn to laugh at yourself, and Count your Blessings!

BAD DAY

A little guy is sitting at the bar just staring at his drink for half an hour when this big trouble-making biker steps next to him, grabs his drink, gulps it down in one swig and then turns to the guy with a menacing stare as if to say, "What'cha gonna do about it?"

The poor little guy starts crying.

"Come on, man. I was just giving you a hard time," the biker says. "I didn't think you'd cry. I can't stand to see a man crying."

"This is the worst day of my life," says the little guy between sobs. "I can't do anything right. I overslept and was late to an important meeting, so my boss fired me. When I went to the parking lot, I found my car was stolen, and I don't have any insurance. I left my wallet in the cab I took home. I found my wife in bed with the gardener, and my dog bit me. So I came to this bar trying to work up the courage to put an end to my life, and then you show up and drink the darn poison."

CUCKOO

Sally, a contestant on *Who Wants to be a Millionaire?* had reached the final plateau. If she answered the next question correctly, she would win $1,000,000. If she answered incorrectly, she would pocket only the $500,000 milestone money.

And as she suspected it would be, the million-dollar question was no pushover.

It was, "Which of the following species of birds does not build its own nest but instead lays its eggs in the nests of other birds?

Is it:

A.) the condor

B.) the buzzard

C.) the cuckoo

D.) the vulture

The woman was put on the spot. She did not know the answer. She had used up her 50/50 lifeline and her Ask-the-Audience lifeline. All that remained for her was the Phone-a-Friend Lifeline. She hoped she would not have to use it because her friend was, well, a blonde. But she had no alternative.

She called her friend and gave her the question and the four choices. The blonde responded unhesitatingly: "That's easy. The answer is C: the cuckoo."

The contestant had to make a decision and make it fast. She considered employing a reverse strategy and giving Meredith any answer except the one that her friend had given her. And considering her friend was a blonde that would seem to be the logical thing to do. But her friend had responded with such confidence, such certitude, that the contestant could not help but be convinced.

"I need an answer," said Meredith.

Crossing her fingers, the contestant said, "C: The cuckoo."

"Is that your final answer?"

"Yes, that is my final answer."

And Meredith replied, "That answer is…absolutely correct! You're now a millionaire!"

Three days later, the contestant hosted a party for her family and friends, including the blonde who had helped her win the million dollars.

"Susan, I just don't know how to thank you," said the contestant. How did you happen to know the right answer?"

"Oh, come on," said the blonde. "Everybody knows that cuckoos don't build nests. They live in clocks."

Sally fainted.

WONDERS OF THE WORLD

A group of students were asked to list what they thought were the present "Seven Wonders of the World."

Though there were some disagreements, the following received the most votes:

1. Egypt's Great Pyramids
2. The Taj Majal
3. The Grand Canyon
4. The Panama Canal
5. The Empire State Building
6. St. Peter's Basilica
7. China's Great Wall

While gathering the votes, the teacher noted that one student had not finished her paper yet. So she asked the girl if she was having trouble with her list.

The girl replied, "Yes, a little. I couldn't quite make up my mind because there are so many."

The teacher said, "Well, tell us what you have, and maybe we can help."

The girl hesitated, and then read, "I think the 'Seven Wonders of the World' are:

2. To see …
3. To hear …

4. To touch…

5. To feel…

6. To laugh…

7. To love…

The room was so quiet you could have heard a pin drop.

The things we overlook as simple and ordinary and what we take for granted are truly wondrous!

The greatest and number one of all the "Wonders of the World" is:

God's amazing Love for mankind in sending His only Son Jesus to set us free and give us everlasting lives. Amen!

A gentle reminder:

The most precious things in life cannot be built by hand or bought by man.

JUST A TAP ON THE SHOULDER

A passenger in a taxi leaned over to ask the driver a question and tapped him on the shoulder.

The driver screamed, lost control of the cab, nearly hit a bus, drove up to the curb, and stopped just inches from a large plate glass window.

For a few moments everything was silent in the cab, and then, the still shaking driver said, "I'm sorry, but you scared the daylights out of me!"

The frightened passenger apologized to the driver and said he didn't realize a mere tap on the shoulder could frighten him so much.

The driver replied, "No, No, I'm sorry, it's entirely my fault.

Today is my first day driving a cab. I've been driving a hearse for the last 25 years."

MY FAVORITES INDEX

Page # 36 Subject Female Driver

Page # 49 Subject The Suit

Page # 59 Subject Did you Know?

Page # 62 Subject The Dinner

Page # 72 Subject Sniffer

Page # 79 Subject Leroy / Leighroy

Page # 86 Subject Local Bar Sues Church

Page # 117 Subject Marriage Seminar

Page # 126 Subject The Note

Page # 130 Subject Mom for Dinner

Page # 137 Subject Living Will

Page # 149 Subject Mood Ring

Page # 201 Subject Not about You

Page # 206 Subject Ex-wife revenge

Page # 231 Subject We survived

Page # 235 Subject Impact

Page # 240 Subject Listening to God

Page # 256 Subject Devil + the Duck

Page # 273 Subject The other is the Husband

Page # 286 Subject Random Acts of Kindness

Page # 298 Subject Tap on Shoulder

Page #_____ Subject_______________________________

Page #_____ Subject_______________________________

Page #_____ Subject_______________________________

Volume II coming soon!

listen|imagine|view|experience

AUDIO BOOK DOWNLOAD INCLUDED WITH THIS BOOK!

In your hands you hold a complete digital entertainment package. Besides purchasing the paper version of this book, this book includes a free download of the audio version of this book. Simply use the code listed below when visiting our website. Once downloaded to your computer, you can listen to the book through your computer's speakers, burn it to an audio CD or save the file to your portable music device (such as Apple's popular iPod) and listen on the go!

How to get your free audio book digital download:

1. Visit www.tatepublishing.com and click on the e|LIVE logo on the home page.
2. Enter the following coupon code: 43cc-6c4e-8d84-f350-a887-e4f6-5903-8c71
3. Download the audio book from your e|LIVE digital locker and begin enjoying your new digital entertainment package today!